ECE/HBP/78

ECONOMIC COMMISSION FOR EUROPE
Geneva

# Rent policy in ECE countries

*Synthesis report*
*on*
*The Seminar held in Amsterdam (Netherlands),*
*27-31 October 1986*

*prepared by*
*L. BUCKERS and M. SEVERIJN (Netherlands)*

**UNITED NATIONS**
New York, 1990

## NOTE

The designations employed and the presentation of material in this publication do not imply the expression of any opinion whatsoever on the part of the Secretariat of the United Nations concerning the legal status of any country, territory, city or area or of its authorities, or concerning the delimitation of its frontiers or boundaries.

\*

\*    \*

Symbols of United Nations documents are composed of capital letters combined with numerals. Mention of such a symbol denotes a reference to a United Nations document.

\*

\*    \*

ECE/HBP/78

UNITED NATIONS PUBLICATION

*Sales No.* E.90.II.E.29

ISBN 92-1-116486-9

02300P

# PREFACE

Rent policy has been on the agenda of the ECE Committee on Housing, Building and Planning since its inception in the late 1940s. In the early years, rents were strictly controlled as a measure, *inter alia*, for curbing speculation and for keeping costs of living down in a situation of acute housing shortage. Rent levels, therefore, did not usually correspond to the real use-value of dwellings. This situation led in turn to the inefficient use and uneven distribution of the existing housing stock among different income and social groups, and to the reduced mobility of the population, with negative effects on national economies.

For the 1980s, an increased awareness has been observed in many ECE countries with regard to the negative effects of rent controls and subsidies. It has been realized that adequate rent levels may stimulate investment in new housing or in modernization, and that maintenance and repair as well as quality of housing in general are directly related to the development of rents. In an increasing number of countries, it has been recognized that public financial resources used to keep rent levels low have limits and that it is important to attempt to increase the share of those households which can afford to pay higher rents. A new situation has thus arisen wherein rent policies are aimed at gradually easing rent controls while charging economically viable rents without, however, losing sight of the needs of specific groups of the population.

This upsurge of interest in rent policy has been reflected in the work of the ECE Committee on Housing, Building and Planning. In 1981, the Working Party on Housing selected rent policy as a major area of concern to be studied in its own right. National monographs on rent policies were prepared and an in-depth discussion was held at the twelfth session of the Working Party in 1984.

The ECE Seminar on Rent Policy was held in Amsterdam (Netherlands) in October 1986. The present report contains a synthesis of the documentation prepared for and discussed at the Seminar. It was compiled by the host-country delegation, in collaboration with the ECE secretariat. A draft of the report was circulated for comment from 1989 to 1990. This final report takes account of comments received up to 30 March 1990.

# CONTENTS

# INTRODUCTION

## A. The call for a seminar

This report deals with government policies on rental dwellings in ECE member countries. The last ECE study of rent policies dates back to 1953.[1] Rent policies were later discussed by the ECE Committee on Housing, Building and Planning as part of a broad range of subjects. In 1981 the Working Party on Housing decided to take up rental housing policies again.

After the discussion of a paper on rent policies prepared by the delegation of the Netherlands, Governments were invited to prepare monographs describing the situations in their respective countries. On the basis of this material, rapporteurs from Belgium, the Netherlands and the Union of Soviet Socialist Republics prepared comprehensive papers that were taken up at the twelfth session of the Working Party in 1984. On that occasion, it was decided to hold a seminar on rent policies. The Seminar was organized to offer participants an opportunity to exchange information, compare experiences and elicit views on rent policies. Discussion of how rent prices were fixed for newly built dwellings, how rent-price adjustments were made and their impact on investments, maintenance and affordability were among the subjects covered. Also on the agenda was the influence of rent policies on the housing market and housing distribution. At the invitation of the Government of the Netherlands, the Seminar was held in Amsterdam in October 1986. It was preceded by a study tour.

The Seminar was attended by representatives of the following countries: Belgium; Bulgaria; Czech and Slovak Federal Republic; Denmark; Finland; France; German Democratic Republic; Germany, Federal Republic of; Hungary; Italy; Netherlands; Norway; Spain; Sweden; Switzerland; United Kingdom; and Yugoslavia. Representatives of the following international non-governmental organizations also participated: International Co-operative Alliance (ICA); International Association for the Development and Management of Existing and New Towns (INTA); International Federation for Housing and Planning (IFHP); International Union of Architects (UIA); International Union of Tenants (IUT); International Real Estate Federation (FIABCI); and International Real Property Union (IRPU).

Three themes had been chosen for discussion, and rapporteurs had prepared discussion papers as follows:

Theme I: The role of rent policies within the framework of general policies: Mr. Boukobza (France) and Mr. E. Federov (USSR);

Theme II: Socio-economic aspects of rent policies: Mr. S. Hillmann (German Democratic Republic) and Mr. J. Samson (Netherlands);

Theme III: Legal and contractual aspects of rent policy: Mr. P. Dufranne (Belgium) and Mr. P. Holczer (Hungary).

## B. Problem definition and approach to the rent-policy project

All ECE countries have some form of rent policy. Moreover, the attitude of public authorities towards the rental sector is changing in many countries. This was the reason why an exchange of information on ways to tackle the main problems was expected to provide new insights. The rent-policy project was intended to provide information on:

(a) The way in which rent policies in the various ECE countries are organized and function;

(b) The nature and scope of the main problems in the field of housing in respective countries;

(c) The way in which rent policies are used by countries to solve the problems mentioned above.

The material in this report was drawn from the monographs prepared by the various countries, the Seminar papers and discussions during the Seminar as well as available literature in the field (*inter alia*, the *Annual Bulletin of Housing and Building Statistics for Europe* and the *1982 Statistical Yearbook*).

## C. Motives for public intervention in housing

In all countries that reported, public authorities play a role in the housing of their citizens. It is not surprising that this be standard practice in the centrally-planned countries of eastern Europe, because of the pre-eminent position of the State in the direction of economic affairs. However, such intervention is probably less readily understood in the countries of western Europe and North America, where market forces are assumed to prevail in the production of dwellings.

To explain why market-economy countries would be concerned about housing, it is sufficient simply to point to the social importance of this sector and to the enduring quality and permanence of the housing stock. There are also macro-economic considerations. Several motives for State intervention are examined below.

---

[1] *Rent Policies in European Countries*, Geneva, August 1953 (E/ECE/170; E/ECE/IM/HOU/44).

## THE SIGNIFICANCE OF HOUSING

Shelter is a basic necessity of life. The way in which this need is met has far-reaching ramifications. The quality of the shelter available affects public health and has an important impact on the productivity and self-development of each citizen, which in turn affects society as a whole. Moreover, housing can have external ripple effects which influence and enhance prosperity. Housing is thus a vital issue in domestic economic policy. It is a key instrument in the distribution and creation of national wealth and well-being.

In many countries public authorities in the field of housing act primarily in response to problems of scarcity of dwelling supply. They also look to measures that will guard against the rising costs of inflation. It is considered normal practice to provide some means of protection to tenants against arbitrary termination of lease agreements and against interim rent-price increases. On the other hand, in order to attract and hold investors, the returns have to be adequately high, and this puts upward pressure on rents. Indeed, a commercial investor expects returns which match possible returns on alternative investments. Such returns are normally calculated in terms of rent yield, but an increase in property value (capital gains) is often an important factor as well. With respect to the supply and demand of dwellings, the housing consumers' interest in affordable rent prices must be balanced against the cost of attracting capital investment for dwelling production.

National authorities regulate and stimulate housing because free-market influences do not result in an acceptable housing situation for all segments of the population. Among reasons why the mechanism does not function ideally, the long lifetime of housing and its immobility or site-specific quality weigh heavily.

## SITE LOCATION

Housing supply is site-specific. People seeking housing often have to move to a place where adequate accommodation is available. Since relocation is a drastic step, people who already have a dwelling are unlikely to move to another dwelling unless there are compelling reasons for doing so. This is so not only because of the financial implications (moving and installations costs), which may be onerous, but also because relocating usually means a change of surroundings. The distribution of housing supply is thus more complicated than the supply of other products.

The location of a dwelling has a great bearing on its market value. Residential quality is thus strongly influenced by the surroundings of dwellings. The surroundings have both physical (landscape, infrastructure, buildings) and social dimensions (neighbours, friends, jobs). Dwelling location has a marked influence on the external effects of housing. Although location is taken into account in housing supply, the producer often has little control over this aspect of housing quality.

The fact that dwellings are fixed in place on the one hand, and the fact that people may have limited mobility on the other, make it difficult to arrange the supply of dwellings optimally so that the costs of housing match income possibilities or so that housing consumption is balanced with housing supply. To attain such an equilibrium, people would have to move if, for instance, there were a change in income or family composition. In the absence of intervention by public authorities, this mobility is very rarely attained. Groups with high incomes tend to hang on to their low-priced dwellings and the elderly, whose children have left home, continue to live in dwellings that are large enough for a growing family. This situation forces young people just entering the housing market and those with low incomes to compete for available dwellings which may be new and expensive, while young families with children may suffer overcrowding.

## DWELLING PERMANENCE

The long duration or useful lifetime of dwellings makes the housing market behave like a stock market, whose supply includes dwellings of various ages. Housing markets often respond slowly to changes in supply and demand. If, for instance, expensive dwellings are introduced to the market during an economic recession, they will not be let at optimal prices. Thus such dwellings might remain vacant while at the same time supply shortages may exist in other segments of the housing market. This is the risk taken when the production is programmed for the construction of expensive new dwellings built with a view to long chains of sequential habitation.

In many countries the public authorities set limits on price increases in the rental dwelling stock so that the current price bears some relationship to the original rent price. The rent-price level of housing produced in different periods of time is often quite unequal because of the rising trend of production costs. This situation leads to marked differences in rent prices which may have no connection with the actual value of the dwelling offered. Old rental dwellings of high quality may thus remain low-priced while new dwellings will be relatively expensive because it is necessary to cover their higher, recent construction costs.

While a dwelling calls for a considerable investment input, this is offset by its durability. There are explanations for the large amount of capital investment required: production must take place on the site where the dwellings will be used; the building industry is more labour-intensive than most other industries; finally, there is a tendency towards higher and higher quality requirements. High costs take their toll when the dwelling is completed. New dwellings are usually the most expensive housing available. This factor also tends to inhibit tenant mobility.

Another housing problem directly linked to the income of tenants is the fact that the housing market can behave like a stock market. The annual addition to the market amounts at the very most to only a few percentage points. Thus distribution of housing is strongly dependent on the price structure of the existing housing stock.

The long lifetime of dwellings means that not only the immediate consumers must be satisfied with the quality offered, but future generations must likewise find satisfaction. Nevertheless, qualitative demands made on dwellings by users, whether collectively or individually, often change at a faster rate than the aging process of housing. Thus, even though they may be physically sound and the capital cost has not yet been entirely written off, certain dwellings may no longer meet the requirements of housing consumers.

With most consumer goods, when they cease to match new quality requirements, the new requirements are satisfied only when the old stock has been retired or upgraded. Renewal of stock in other economic sectors may be a matter of years. In the case of housing, it is necessary to count in decades. Where housing is concerned, changes in demand may affect supply only after long periods of time. Overall quality improvements can only come about gradually. The external negative effects of bad-quality new dwellings continue to exert an influence for a considerable period of time. This is why in many countries public authorities have been charged with the long-term task of watching over the interests of housing consumers.

### Macro-economic considerations

Dwellings are an important factor in the economy in terms not only of quantity but also of quality. Governments can promote employment by stimulating the construction of housing.

In countries where the rental sector is large, rent prices will have an impact on wages. Accordingly, if rent prices are modest, wage demands should be lower. Conversely, increases in rent prices often lead to demands for higher wages. For this reason, wage and price policies have often incorporated legal measures to curb rising rent prices. When rents rise during a period of rising construction and operating costs, the outlook for tenants may be less favourable.

Individual rent subsidies (personalized subsidy) and object subsidies (subsidies attached to the "brick") stimulate demand for high-quality dwellings and render higher-quality dwellings accessible to larger numbers of people. Subsidies thus constitute a buffer against sharp declines in demand during periods of economic stagnation. Public financial aid can make rental dwellings affordable during a period of decreasing real income. Not only does this serve the cause of public welfare, but the State may also have a financial stake in averting bankruptcy on the part of lessors.

### Forms of public intervention

The influence of housing policy on the housing market can take various forms. In most ECE countries there will probably be more than one form. Interventions usually cover:

(a) Regulation of rent prices;

(b) Regulation of the legal relationship between tenant and lessor (for the tenants' protection);

(c) Public aid for dwelling construction (object subsidies) or for tenants (subject subsidies);

(d) Quality requirements;

(e) Dwelling distribution.

These elements are often interrelated. The regulation of rent-price increases can protect tenants. In turn, the existence of such measures can serve as arguments for subsidizing lessors as well. Governments can set quality requirements or attach distribution conditions to subsidies. Below, this paper will discuss principles which might guide policy related to the setting of rent prices.

When a Government provides subsidies in order to guarantee affordable rent prices for lower income groups, there are obviously conditions attached to the rent prices to be agreed upon. In a system of free-floating rent prices, there is no guarantee that dwellings earmarked for subsidies will remain within the reach of the people for whom they were intended. It sometimes happens that public authorities provide subsidies in order to stimulate dwelling production. In such cases, there is probably less justification for regulating rent prices.

### D. Structure of the report

The report begins with a summary which, in addition to summarizing the report, presents an outline of recent developments in rent policy in the ECE region. Each chapter starts with a short theoretical introduction. Policy instruments are described and analysed. Comparisons between countries are made.

Chapter 1, on rent prices and subsidy policies, discusses classic price theory, cost-price rents, quality-based rents and income-based rents.

Chapter 2, on the housing stock and dwelling production, deals with ways in which building initiatives may be directed, and explores various ideas concerning the desired composition of the dwelling stock. Data are presented on the size and formation of the rental housing sector in each of the ECE countries.

Rent-price policy and dwelling exploitation is the subject of chapter 3, which discusses ways in which public authorities, through subsidies and price regulation, influence the relation between exploitation costs and investment returns. A brief description is given of the situation in each ECE country.

Under rent-price policy and dwelling quality (chapter 4), the discussion focuses on the setting of rent prices for newly built dwellings as well as how corrections of historically set rent prices are made using dwelling valuation systems. A country-by-country analysis is given.

Chapter 5 deals with ways in which rent-price policy can ease the housing burden by distributing costs according to income, whether through individualized rent subsidies or income-related rents. The situation in each country is described.

Rent legislation (chapter 6) describes policies governing legal relations between tenants and lessors, in particular contract procedures, termination of leases and distribution of maintenance obligations. Each ECE country is reported on in this section.

# SUMMARY

## A. General

Rental dwellings constitute an important part of the total housing stock in all ECE countries. Moreover, by means of subsidies and price regulation, all ECE Governments influence demand development as well as operational aspects. Such public intervention affects not only the quantity of rental dwellings produced, but also home improvement and maintenance activities.

Public direction of housing is a fundamental government task in the centrally-planned economies of eastern Europe, where the State takes charge of providing housing for the entire population. Dwelling production follows a formal State plan. Available dwellings are distributed in accordance with directives issued by the public authorities. Rent prices are fixed on the basis of government decisions.

To date, the policy of the countries of eastern Europe has been to keep the price of housing low for everyone. Rent prices range from 2 per cent to 5 per cent of household expenses. This low percentage is maintained only through a vast subsidization system. In most of the countries reporting, the income of the tenant is not taken into consideration; hence, high income groups also benefit from housing subsidies. Notwithstanding the large-scale State-operated housing system, eastern European countries also have a large owner-occupied sector. In Bulgaria and Hungary for instance, a considerable amount of dwelling production depends on private initiatives.

In western ECE countries, the effects of the market mechanism are mitigated by public intervention. Housing in the market-economy countries is subject to a mixture of public regulation and market influences. Government is concerned with housing subsidization policies for covering various elements: construction and exploitation of housing; protection of tenants against unreasonable rent prices; and aid to specific demographic groups. Consequently, housing policy in the market-economy countries is only partly determined by the market forces of supply and demand.

Quality requirements imposed by housing authorities may exert upward pressure on rent prices. Public health considerations and general well-being are factors in setting minimum standards with regard to the number of rooms, space per person, sanitary facilities, heating, lighting, insulation, etc. As quality standards rise, so too do construction and operating costs. Quality requirements can therefore make housing expensive. When this happens, housing authorities may be called upon to fill the rent-price gap that reflects costs on the one hand, and affordability or income on the other.

State aid may take the form of object and subject subsidies for housing. Object subsidies work by lowering the rent price of dwellings as a block. Such subsidies may be keyed, for instance, to the average income of tenants in a target group. Subject subsidies or personalized rent subsidies are intended to bring the cost of housing within reach of individual tenants or occupants, and thus help balance outlay and income. Where rent prices are controlled, the Government determines the conditions and extent by which any increases may be allowed.

In many countries object subsidies are applied to compensate lessors for the disadvantages of price regulation or control. This form of subsidy is also applied in order to reach social objectives, for instance in connection with urban renewal policy. This report deals with the object subsidy only in so far as it has a bearing on rent prices. Financial aspects have already been dealt with under the ECE project on Financing of Housing.

The policies for the distribution of housing and the determination of rent prices in the social housing sector in the market-economy countries of the ECE region resemble those covering the rental housing stock in the countries of eastern Europe. Both sets of countries direct support towards population groups in a weak position in the housing market (for example, the elderly, the handicapped, students, people with low incomes, *et al.*). Governments within both politico-economic systems may impose limits on possible increases in rent prices, in order to protect tenants and curb inflation. The resemblance should not be too surprising: the reasons for public intervention are essentially the same in both groups of countries; and there is no great divergence in terms of objectives.

## B. Rent-price policy and dwelling exploitation

In many ECE countries, the aim is to make the rent price match the real running costs, at least for part of the housing stock. Any increase in expenditures incurred by the housing manager must be matched by increases in rent prices. In many countries there is a difference between the cost of housing and the rent price charged to tenants for such housing. This difference may be covered by object subsidies. These may help cover part of the expenses met in allocating funds for building. Interest subsidies exist in: Austria; Belgium; Denmark; France; Finland; Germany, Federal Republic of; and Sweden. Subsidies are applied in Ireland, the Netherlands and the United Kingdom to cover running costs.

In the United Kingdom, for instance, the amount of the subsidy is fixed so that lessors of social housing function somewhat independently of the central Government. With regard to cost control, the State is not obliged to issue strict prescriptions governing rent policy. There are other examples (e.g. Ireland) where the level of State support depends on the rent prices calculated. Such financial involvement suggests that rent-price policy exerts a strong influence.

In the countries of eastern Europe, Governments provide large-scale object subsidies as a means of keeping rent prices low. In several of these countries, rent prices have remained unchanged for a long time. Rent prices of privately owned dwellings are aligned with those of the public sector.

In most western ECE countries, a distinction is made between public and private sectors in terms of methods by which rent prices are set and adjusted. In the private rental sector, tenants and lessors negotiate the rent price (sometimes collectively). Often, however, a maximum rent price is set by law, in order to protect tenants against unreasonably high rent prices. The same applies to rent-price adjustments.

Rent-price policy for the private sector does not, in general, deal with running costs, the assumption being that the commercial lessor will not need protection against unremunerative rents. If investment returns do become too small, private offers will be withdrawn. The supply then becomes quite uniform, an effect which is detrimental to the functioning of the housing market.

In the non-profit housing sector in the western ECE countries, there is usually a direct relationship between rent price and running costs. The reason for this is the financial involvement of the Government in running social housing. This involvement (through subsidies) diminishes over a period of time. A regular fixed reduction in subsidies granted for operation or exploitation means that the State budget for housing will eventually have some relief and not be overburdened. The disadvantage of this approach is that rent prices may rise to compensate for subsidy reductions. This could exert pressure to move out on the original target group aided.

If rent prices are not adjusted when capital charges and running costs rise, the gap will have to be covered by greater and greater subsidies. In all countries of the ECE region—both east and west—any long-term increase in housing expenses is unacceptable for the State. Ways and means are sought to bring rent prices into line with actual costs, without compromising the social nature of housing benefits.

## C. Rent-price policy and dwelling quality

In a number of ECE countries, housing quality has an important bearing on the rent price set. To determine what rent price is justified for a given level of quality, some instrument is needed for assessing quality. Such instruments must be objective, yet take into account perceived preferences of housing occupants.

In all the countries of eastern Europe, the quality of a rental dwelling (measured in greater or less detail) is expressed as the rent price paid by the occupants. Floor space and the level of equipment provided are the quality characteristics considered most relevant. In this respect, there is no distinction to be made among the various rental sectors.

In many countries of western Europe, rent price is related to dwelling quality in two ways:

(a) Dwelling quality becomes a factor as a result of disputes over rent prices. This applies to the whole rental sector in Finland, Netherlands and Turkey and to part of the rental stock in: Germany, Federal Republic of; Ireland; Norway; Switzerland; and the United Kingdom;

(b) Dwelling quality plays a role in the setting of the rent price and in any adjustments thereof or with regard to disputes. This applies to the entire rental sector in France and Norway and to part of the rental stock in Austria, Portugal, Sweden and the United Kingdom.

For the entire rental sector in Belgium, Denmark and Spain, there is no direct relationship between rent price and dwelling quality. This is true for only part of the rental stock in the following countries: Austria; Germany, Federal Republic of; Ireland; Portugal; and Switzerland.

## D. Rent-price policy and the housing burden

Good housing can be expensive. Many people have to set aside a large part of their income for housing expenditures. People with very low incomes cannot afford decent housing if they are required to pay the total cost unaided. When a Government wishes to guarantee that the entire population is decently lodged, two questions arise: What is the maximum proportion of personal income that people should spend on housing? And: What minimum quality requirements should apply to housing?

With regard to the share of personal income earmarked for housing, this question is relevant to public authorities because of concern for lower income groups. The lowest income groups would spend at least one third of family income on housing if there were no government intervention. Expenditures of such proportions do not leave enough money to cover living costs. This is the reason why, in a number of ECE countries, Governments subsidize subsistence tenants. Subsidies usually cover the difference between the rent paid by assisted tenants and the actual cost of the housing provided.

A technical term to describe the relation between income and housing expenses is the housing burden ratio. The prevailing political and social policies determine both the maximum housing burden ratio and the minimum quality requirements. The financial leeway enjoyed by the public authorities also plays a role in determining this ratio. In many countries, an average housing burden ratio of 25 per cent is considered acceptable. Even so, housing is the heaviest expenditure item in the budget of most consumers.

The policy in Belgium, Ireland, and Portugal is to set the rent price in relation to the tenant's income. The criteria for such aid in Portugal is household size and income level. In Belgium, income is the only criterion. The criteria for Ireland were not reported. In all three countries, however, the rent price paid by the tenant is adjusted if there are changes in the tenant's income. An increase in income results in an increase in the rent price. In Belgium, there is an explicit provision that as soon as income surpasses a given maximum, the tenant is obliged to quit the public housing sector.

In most ECE countries, there is a ceiling for maximum rent increases in the private rental sector as well. It was not clear whether this limit bore any relation to income development. In the Netherlands, when setting the maximum annual rent increase, any changes in purchasing power are taken into account. In France and Sweden, there is a system of collective negotiations between tenants' and lessors' organizations. In Finland, negotiations take place during the process of preparing the Government's yearly decision on the rent level and its increase. It was not clear whether income development plays a role in these negotiations.

Many ECE countries provide object subsidies as a way of adding to the number of rental dwellings for which the initial rent price is below cost price. In this way, affordable accommodation is made available. Object subsidies are used to keep rents low, especially in the countries of eastern Europe where the rent price does not need to relate to the costs of housing services or a tenant's income. Rent prices in these countries do not usually cover running costs. In recent years, however, there has been a tendency to raise rents to the level which would cover running costs (but excluding capital costs).

Many ECE countries have a policy of lower housing expenditures for lower income groups. This is done through individualized subsidies (subject subsidies). These subsidies may apply to the entire housing stock, to the rental stock only, or to parts thereof. In Spain and Switzerland, individualized subsidies are applied only to the social rental stock. Individualized subsidies apply to the entire social rental stock in the following countries: Austria; Denmark; Finland; German Democratic Republic; Germany, Federal Republic of; Hungary; Netherlands; Norway; Sweden; and the United Kingdom. In France and the Federal Republic of Germany, there are also certain assistance benefits for owner-occupied dwellings as well.

There are various criteria for granting a subsidy and for fixing the amount. The most important criterion is the income of the head of the household or the entire household income. Some countries have different subsidy systems for different groups, sometimes varying according to the amount of public aid. In Denmark, a distinction is made between pensioners and other households. In Finland, students are also a separate group for subsidy purposes. The United Kingdom has two systems: if the subsidy covering rent does not bring the tenants above the poverty line, there is resort to an additional subsidy (under the public assistance scheme). Sweden has three subsidy schemes: one for pensioners and two for other households. There is a State subsidy computed on the basis of the number of children and a combined State/municipality subsidy based on income and housing expenditure. Switzerland has two forms of subsidy: one is earmarked to aid the elderly, handicapped and disabled; the second is applied to other households in need. A rent-subsidy mechanism and a rent-correction mechanism are applied to large families in the German Democratic Republic and in Poland respectively. Hungary has a subsidy for pensioners.

The most common criteria for establishing the level of subject subsidies are: income level (of the head of the household or total household); the amount of the rent price; household size (or number of children); dwelling size; and dwelling quality.

## E. Rent legislation

In most ECE countries, rent legislation has an equalizing influence that helps reduce inherent disparities between parties to a lease contract. National authorities may impose coercive laws to protect the weaker party. It is useful to distinguish between supplementary legislation and coercive law in this context. Supplementary legislation may contain provisions that apply in the absence of a prior agreement between the parties; coercive law prescribes compulsory arrangements to which the parties are obliged to adhere. The legal protection of tenants may be assured by stipulations regarding termination of the lease contract (termination notice) and covering allocation of maintenance tasks as well as sublet and co-tenancy possibilities. Failure to comply with an agreement may render the agreement null and void. In some countries it is possible to overrule coercive stipulations in rent legislation if organizations of tenants and lessors so agree, the assumption being that tenants acting collectively have sufficient negotiating power to render superfluous the protection offered by coercive laws.

The extent of public intervention tends to reflect not only prevailing views concerning ownership rights but also supply and demand ratios. In the western ECE countries, the scope of public intervention in relations between lessors and tenants varies widely. In the countries of eastern Europe, the emphasis on protection of tenants has made the position of the private lessor relatively weak. In some cases, it is not even possible for private parties to let housing space.

In several countries, special bodies have been set up to deal with disputes between tenants and lessors. These bodies offer the parties a possibility to settle their differences through low-cost arbitration procedures. The informality of the process means that tenants and lessors do not need to engage legal counsel. Furthermore, such procedures relieve the more formal judicial machinery of an unnecessary burden although there are usually provisions for appealing against the decisions of the special rent courts.

## F. Recent developments

In a number of ECE market-economy countries, the public authorities have been reducing their role and tending to withdraw in favour of private initiatives. Public-sector support peaked during the early 1970s and then began to drop as the countries headed into an economic slowdown. Tax receipts were dwindling while public expenditure in the sphere of social services rose, leading to an untenable situation. A correction was essential. Public expenditure had to be reduced or at least its growth trend had to be curtailed. Housing was not exempt from the squeeze. While the existence of budgetary constraints did not obviate the need to provide housing, the tasks were redefined and thus the policies also changed.

In the centrally-planned countries of eastern Europe, there is also a tendency to reduce public housing expenditures and to balance this by increasing the share of housing costs borne by housing consumers. While State intervention is not the question in the countries of eastern Europe, the policy trend is nevertheless similar to that of western Europe. The impact of heavier and heavier housing costs on national budgets is one reason underlying the impulse to stimulate private initiative and to let rent prices rise. In the countries of eastern Europe, owing to the generally improved standards of living, there are now population groups which can afford better, more expensive housing. This has somewhat lessened the need to support public housing.

A high level of dwelling production coupled with considerable object subsidies (so as to keep rental expenditures low) place a heavy burden on State budgets. This policy direction is increasingly perceived as a problem in socialist countries. The tendency is now to bring rents more into line with the real cost of housing-stock exploitation. Likewise, western ECE countries are reducing object subsidies and letting rent prices paid by consumers rise. In both the socialist and the market-economy countries of the region, the current policy is to attune rent prices to running costs.

Many ECE countries have shifted away from object subsidies in favour of subject subsidies. Financial aid to individual householders is seen by Governments as being easier on State budgets than object subsidies as a means of lowering rent prices. However, while the subject subsidy has the advantage of allocating public financial support where the need is greatest, it has certain inherent disadvantages. In general, individual subject subsidies cannot be assured on a long-term basis. Whenever budgetary constraints lead to reductions of individualized subsidies, the impact falls immediately on the weakest population groups.

Withdrawal of government financial support to housing has an effect on dwelling affordability, especially that of newly built dwellings. Mobility and housing distribution becomes more restricted if the dwelling-stock growth ceases. In order to stimulate mobility, several countries have policies which link rent prices to dwelling quality or occupant income.

In many ECE countries, housing shortages have led to a more intensified use of the existing housing stock. There is a tendency to let market forces of supply and demand affect rent prices as Governments exercise less influence on rent prices. Moreover, a shrinking public purse has reduced the possibilities of investing in housing. As the supply of housing grows, managers are obliged to make greater concessions in order to find tenants. Furthermore, freedom of action improves as public authorities withdraw. Private housing addresses middle and higher income groups, i.e. the most attractive part of the market. If the Government does not intervene, people with low incomes compete for a limited supply of low-quality but relatively expensive rental dwellings.

In general, throughout the ECE region the production of rental dwellings has dwindled while the owner-occupied sector has expanded. Several countries are pursuing an active policy of selling off part of their stock of social rental dwellings to occupants. As the stock of cheap rental dwellings shrinks, the risk of supply shortages of dwellings for low-income groups increases.

# Chapter 1

## RENT-PRICE AND SUBSIDY POLICIES: STARTING POINTS

## I. PRELIMINARY REMARKS

### A. Classical price theory

Price formation in a market economy is the result of dynamic interaction between supply and demand. Economic theory illustrates this balance using a system of co-ordinates plotting the prices of goods or services against the corresponding supply offered. One trend line shows a curve representing the effect of prices on consumption; a second curve shows the relation between prices and production. The two curves bear an inverse relation to one another: the lower the price; the lower the production, which leads in turn to a shorter supply. Conversely, a drop in prices makes purchase and consumption more attractive and hence demand becomes greater. A shortage of supply can lead consumers to bid against one another in order to obtain scarce goods or services. This competition drives prices up, which has the effect of stimulating production and hence engenders a growth in supply. According to classical price theory, the market mechanism yields a balanced price at the intersection of the demand and supply curves.

### B. Housing market prices

The model described in the preceding paragraph does not lend itself readily to housing-market applications. One reason for this is that the product varies greatly in quality. One way to resolve the problem of diversity of quality would be to ascribe price formation for dwellings of varying quality to separate submarkets. When supply and demand are well balanced on the various submarkets, any price differences may be attributed to differences in dwelling quality, in so far as these differences are relevant to consumers. The distribution of dwellings among consumers will be the result of differentiation between rent price and quality on the one hand, and consumer preferences and purchasing power on the other. Those who can pay more may demand higher quality, although they may also be satisfied with less.

Notwithstanding the addition of quality differences to the model, the rent-price mechanism does not function according to the theory described. There is a reason for this. Public authorities influence supply and demand, at least for part of the market. Political decisions can play a role in rent-price formation, and that role can be as important as quality differences and the purchasing power of consumers.

### C. Rent-price policy

If housing were entirely subject to free market forces alone, some population groups would run the risk of not being able to afford housing to meet their needs. For lower income groups, problems arise when income lags behind adjustments in the rent-price level. To alleviate this problem, rent policy in many countries is aimed at fixing rent prices (for at least part of the housing market) lower than market prices for certain income groups. In some cases this means that the rent price is below that required to cover running costs. Thus, the gap is filled with financial aid provided by Governments in the form of object subsidies so that the lessor can meet expenses.

Another way in which a dwelling of reasonable quality may be made affordable for lower income groups is to provide the tenant with a subsidy geared to income criteria (subject subsidies). Many western ECE countries have set up systems of subject subsidies. This solution has the merit of not lowering the general rent-price level, while bringing benefits to those who really need help. To this extent at least, the individual rent subsidy is more effective than an object subsidy.

However, systems of individualized rent subsidies are less appropriate as a steering instrument with regard to the overall rent-price level. For certain economic reasons (for instance, to slow inflation), it may be desirable to steer prices. Many western ECE countries therefore rely on a combination of both types of subsidies. Eastern ECE countries have not developed the use of individualized rent subsidy to any extent.

As a result of the influence of public authorities on rent-price levels (through object and subject subsidy systems), the Government has a direct interest in housing operations. In the case of object subsidies, the Government is interested in increasing rent prices so as to reduce the subsidy. As for subject subsidies, the Government is interested in keeping rent-price increases down, so that subsidies paid on behalf of tenants remain lower. Consequently, in countries where both systems are used in combination, the Government is faced with conflicting interests.

## II. THREE CRITERIA FOR RENT POLICIES

In theory, rent prices may be regulated according to three criteria:

(a) Cost-price rents—the rent price is fixed at a level which covers costs;

(*b*) Quality-based rents—the rent price reflects the quality value;

(*c*) Income-related rents—the rent price depends on the tenant's income.

These elements are often combined in various ways. Policy may then focus on adjustments needed to achieve the desired results. Thus, the most relevant question will be to decide whether housing policy should address the needs of the largest population groups, or the poorest, or should find a balance somewhere in between.

## A. Cost-price rents

Cost-price rents are those rents which yield returns to match the entire cost of construction and operation of the dwelling. The supply of housing becomes a business activity. People seeking dwellings decide how much they are willing or able to pay as rent. Entrepreneurs decide whether a given revenue from rentals will cover investments, maintenance and improvements. Government regulations may fix rent-price ceilings at a level adequate to cover such costs as construction and maintenance. For the lessor, although the costs are covered, the returns are nevertheless circumscribed. The occupants are protected, however, against rent prices that are too high.

### ADVANTAGES AND DISADVANTAGES

Cost-price rents have a disadvantage in that it is difficult to predetermine their precise level and they may bear little relation to the housing market. This can be explained. At the outset of the exploitation of a housing unit it is not always easy to know exactly what rent price will cover all costs. The amortization period is often several decades. Changes in running costs over such a long period cannot be predicted accurately. Estimates must be made of interest rates, fixed and variable changes for services, as well as inflationary trends. In order to attract investors, rent-price calculations also have to show a return on the capital investment. Prediction of this yield is likewise estimated. Moreover, assumptions have to be made as to the possible returns on alternative investments over the same period as well as the proceeds from the eventual sale value of the property. In addition, there is also the problem of how to spread the revenue calculated over the lifetime of the building.

Depending on the assumptions made, the rent price will vary greatly. If events do not turn out as predicted in the calculations, financial losses may ensue for the lessor or tenants may be subject to steep rent increases. If a certain rent price is fixed and unalterable, the lessor runs the risk of seeing costs outweigh returns. Governments can help to solve the problem by the use of subsidies to cover any difference between the costs predicted and the actual costs. Government in a sense then takes upon itself some of the entrepreneurial risks. Another solution is to adjust the rents periodically to bring them in line with the cost of development. Both solutions have the disadvantage of not offering optimal incentives for lessors to keep costs down.

Cost-price rents react more to the cost structure at the time the dwellings are built than to subsequent developments in the housing market. Interest rates are a critical factor in this context. Discrepancies in rent prices for dwellings of equal quality may be attributed to fluctuations in interest rates: for instance, dwellings financed during periods of higher interest rates may be more expensive and hence difficult to let. The lessor will lack flexibility in such a case. If, for instance, in order to make an unlet dwelling more attractive, upgrading measures are introduced, then application of the cost-price principle would simply offset any gains in attractiveness as the rent price must be increased to cover renovation costs. This situation could lead to a downward spiral. Furthermore, if the rent price, once fixed, cannot be raised or lowered in line with changes in market values, good dwellings may be offered cheaper than those which are not as good. Demand will then surge for the dwellings with an artificially low rent price. This disparity can lead to a series of public interventions in the housing field.

Once the free-market mechanism has been eliminated as an instrument for housing distribution, other criteria for allocating dwellings among house-hunters must be found by the authorities concerned. If the rent price remains too low to cover running costs, the problem becomes critical. This is why there is a need for subsidies. Moreover, the propensity to invest slackens if rent prices are held artificially below market values: there is no incentive for entrepreneurs. When rent yields are not linked to quality-based consumer preferences, new housing starts in the rental sector will dry up.

Fluctuations in construction costs can be offset by increasing subsidies during periods of high costs and reducing them when costs are lower. In this way, the rent price asked may be stabilized, albeit at a high level. Governments will be called upon to allocate greater financial resources during times of high interest rates in order to finance rental dwellings, but this is precisely the time when it would be wiser for Governments to restrain making such commitments in order to avoid putting upward pressure on interest rates by borrowing when the money supply is already tight.

In the countries of eastern Europe, cost-price rents have not been considered an acceptable starting-point at which to set rents. Hence, this aspect will not be treated with respect to this group of countries.

## B. Quality-based rents

Quality-based rents are those fixed on the basis of quality factors. To this end, "quality" must be rendered measurable and a formula devised for calculating prices based on quality criteria. For newly built dwellings, the cost price remains a decisive factor, otherwise the supply of new dwellings will shrink. A lessor must be able to cover investment costs and gain an incentive yield through quality-related rent prices.

In order to apply this principle in a flexible manner, quality levels can be identified and maximum rent prices set, instead of setting a fixed, definitive rent price. Tenants and lessors thus have some scope in which to negotiate, the only restriction being that a tenant should not be committed to a price that is deemed unreasonable on the grounds of quality. For a given quality, it is also possible to establish a minimum rent price. Rents below this threshold could be raised so as to streamline rent prices in the housing stock. The field of negotiation between tenants and lessors would then range between the minimum and maximum limits of a rent price justified by housing quality considerations.

### ADVANTAGES

In general, quality-based rent prices promote household mobility. Normally, this way of ascribing rent prices also stimulates efficient management on the part of lessors and prevents the formation of scarcity prices. This observation can be explained.

A clear-cut relation between price and quality stimulates tenant mobility. Tenants who inhabit a cheap but good dwelling are not likely to move out, even if their income rises or their space needs decrease. To move would mean paying more for less value. Cheaper dwellings will thus rarely become available for lower income groups. Furthermore, large dwellings will remain occupied by households which have shrunk in size as children grow up and leave home. Lack of mobility will lead to scarcity in certain sectors at least. Low mobility will make it necessary to resort to expensive new construction in order to house some population groups. When rent prices are based on quality factors, such problems can be avoided. The system of quality-based rent prices rewards lessors who operate efficiently. If their costs are lower than expected in terms of the housing quality offered, then any difference between real costs and anticipated costs enhances their profit margin.

### DISADVANTAGES

Two problems may be cited with regard to quality-based rent prices. One is the difficulty of establishing quality in an objective way. Furthermore, in addition to quality, it may also be desirable to take account of variable costs.

Any register of quality will have a subjective bias. It is not sufficient to measure only the physical elements of a dwelling; the state of maintenance and the surroundings, for example, must also be assessed. It is simply not feasible to take account of an average appreciation of all the relevant factors in such an assessment, not to speak of the preferences of all potential individual tenants.

Furthermore, dwelling construction is a field that is too diversified for any broad scale of standards to be devised that will fit into one single evaluation framework. The consideration of multiple, somewhat subjective elements heightens the likelihood of disputes between tenants and lessors. In order to do justice to all the quality nuances, the system would become quite unwieldy. If the assessment were confined to only some elements of dwelling quality, the system would be easy to apply, but would cease to respond to the great diversity of quality considerations. Somehow, a combination of optimal quality criteria and pragmatic efficiency has to be found.

A problem arises if the value of certain quality elements is not reflected in the rent price. Any feature provided that costs more than the value attributed to it in the quality evaluation becomes a lost asset from the lessor's point of view. The temptation would be to annul such benefits. In addition, there would be some uncertainty concerning adjustments required to compensate for cost increases. Quality-related rent prices could be limited, however, to part of the rental dwelling stock.

## C. Income-related rents

There are various ways of linking rent price to a tenant's income. Relatively very cheap accommodation can be supplied through the use of individualized subsidies. Subject subsidies are applied to fill the gap between a tenant's means and the rent price asked. The object subsidy is also aimed at making a dwelling affordable for the tenants.

### HOUSING FREE OF CHARGE, OR ALMOST

If public authorities choose not to intervene in the housing market or to favour only a small group composed of the financially weakest members of society, they could supply them with acceptable-quality housing free of charge or for almost no charge as a form of charity. Occupants are thus selected according to their lack of means. They would then be required to leave the low-rental unit if their income exceeded a certain ceiling. In such cases, socially assisted housing provides only for the lowest income group.

Such a system is attractive from the viewpoint of control of expenditure. Only those who qualify for assistance can benefit; the financial aid allocated is predetermined. There are disadvantages, however. A high concentration of population stigmatized by low incomes leads to neglect and accelerated decay of the dwelling complex.

The countries of eastern Europe have a policy of extremely low rent prices. As the State is simultaneously the employer, the contractor and the landlord, the authorities can opt for low wages and low prices, including low rent prices. Several centrally-planned countries have a rent policy which is not related to construction or running costs. The State undertakes to cover an important part of housing expenses on the grounds that all citizens are entitled to cheap rents. Income is not necessarily a decisive factor in the allocation of dwelling quality elements. Low rent prices have the advantage of helping to maintain wages at an established level.

In a system of income-related rents, the rent paid by the tenant depends on the household income and other considerations. The dwelling quality offered can also be taken into account. Income-related rent prices are found in a few countries which have a relatively small social-housing rental sector.

### ADVANTAGES AND DISADVANTAGES

Income-related rents promote tenant mobility and allow for orderly financing systems. However, rather an extensive administrative machinery is needed. This will be explained.

Tenants whose income rises can stay in the rental unit by paying a higher rent. They are thus not forced to vacate although they may see an advantage in finding a dwelling where the rent price is not tied to income. When such a tenant vacates the dwelling, it becomes available for tenants who are closer to the minimum. Unlike the system whereby rent prices for an entire housing complex are set for population segments which have minimal purchasing power, income-related rents have the advantage in that admission criteria will be less severe and consequently the population composition more mixed.

Financing and administration of income-related rents lends itself to an orderly system. The number of dwellings available is easy to identify. The level of the average income is known. Thus rent returns can be estimated fairly well.

Income-related rent-price systems make it necessary to maintain an administrative control to monitor tenant income, quality and rent price. Furthermore, tenants may have less incentive to improve their income situation. With income-related rents, the reaction time is somewhat slow when responding to the need to expand the supply of dwellings. In practice, income-related rents are rather rare.

## III. THREE INSTRUMENTS OF RENT-PRICE POLICY: OBJECT SUBSIDIES, SUBJECT SUBSIDIES AND RENT-ADJUSTMENT REGULATION

### A. Object subsidies

In many ECE countries, the Government provides subsidies to fill the gap between the housing costs and the rent price asked. The various forms of object subsidies which are most frequently used will be described below.

Examples of object subsidies include low-interest public loans or subsidies covering the interest on loans granted by traditional lending institutions. Public or semi-public loans have the advantage of forestalling a rise in interest rates which could be triggered by an interest subsidy. In the case of subsidized loans, no attention is usually paid to dwelling quality. The loan normally amounts to a percentage of the cost of acquisition or construction; the balance is financed by the applicant.

Linking the loan to construction costs may incur risks of enhancement of maximum quality or, in effect, higher costs. Many countries impose qualifying conditions in order to counteract this tendency. Such conditions may be all-inclusive and straightforward, or detailed and complicated. In the Federal Republic of Germany, for instance, the qualifications are rather simple: in addition to specifying a maximum surface area, there is also a limit allowance of construction costs per square metre of surface. Furthermore, the minimum requirements are high and the maximum quality level is low. Because the margin between the minimum and maximum is narrow, the lessor of social housing is obliged to build to an optimal cost/quality ratio. In France, Sweden and Finland, to take another example, any investment decision is checked using very complicated calculations.

In many cases, subsidies are degressive. The interest-subsidy contribution per residential building gradually drops over the exploitation period according to a predetermined scale, eventually reaching the current market rate of interest. This method of automatic reduction of subsidies has resulted in substantial rent-price increases in a number of countries. During the 1970s, when inflation rates were lower than the rate calculated when the loans were plotted, the real rent-price increase grew more sharply than expected. When interest subsidies run out, the financial ties between lessors and public authorities are weakened. However, strict rent-price policy and strict controls on dwelling exploitation are not required in order to hold public expenses in check, as the subsidy structure of the loan has been calculated and fixed in advance in such cases.

In the ECE countries of eastern Europe, the authorities provide large-scale object subsidies in order to keep rent prices low. In several countries, rent prices have not changed for many years. Rent prices in the (small) private sector are closely related to those in the public sector because the latter functions as the price-setting leader. During periods when the rate of production of new State-sponsored dwellings is high, the State allocates significant object subsidies in order to keep rent prices low; housing costs then weigh heavily on the public budget. This is increasingly considered a problem in eastern Europe. There is now a move to attune rent prices to the actual costs involved in running a housing complex. In several western ECE countries, an effort is also being made to reduce expenditures incurred in object subsidies by raising rent prices. Hence, both eastern and western ECE countries are developing housing policies that relate rent prices to running costs.

### B. Subject subsidies

The individual or personalized rent subsidy is applied in many countries. Governments provide subsidies to tenants whose incomes are too low for them to be able to afford to pay the full rent price. In some countries, individual rent subsidies are tied as supplements to the system of social allowances. In others, tenants may be entitled to individual rent subsidies irrespective of their source of income.

The question is often raised whether an individual rent subsidy should be considered a housing subsidy or a subsidy within the system of social security. The former seems more likely, as a rent subsidy is earmarked for housing and cannot be spent otherwise. Nevertheless, individual rent subsidies bear some similarity to social security allowances. In countries where such subsidies are applied on a large scale, the subsidy system has a bearing on overall financial policy. Tenants who must rely solely on social security allowances may consider the individual rent subsidy a supplement to their welfare allowance or pension. Moreover, individual rent subsidies are subject to the same rules as social security allowances, whereby any increase in income leads to a reduction of subsidization. It is believed that this qualification

could serve as a disincentive for people who might otherwise make an extra effort to become less dependent on subsidies.

The question of whether the individual rent subsidy falls properly within the domain of housing subsidies or social security aid should be examined in the light of the overall field of housing rather than in terms of the various elements listed above. If the individual rent subsidy is a factor in a system that links together subject subsidies, object subsidies and a rent-price adjustment mechanism, the answer should be clear. If, moreover, it is connected to a dwelling distribution system that makes cheaper dwellings available for lower income groups, then it is unquestionably a housing instrument.

However, if from a pragmatic point of view, there is no tie between housing policy and individual rent subsidies, there may be an argument for viewing rent subsidies as a specific supplement to the allowances paid to tenants burdened with heavy housing expenses. In such a case, the population groups benefiting from an individual rent subsidy will more than likely already be the recipients of an allowance granted on other grounds.

## C. Rent-adjustment regulation

Another form of State intervention in the rental housing sector is the control of changes in rent prices. Rent prices cannot be altered simply according to changes in the housing market. For instance, if the number of people seeking dwellings exceeds the supply of dwellings, on a free market rent prices will rise. In most countries, there is some form of protection for tenants against unlimited rent increases or arbitrary notice to vacate a dwelling.

One intervention leads to another. For instance, if rent controls make the letting of older dwellings non-remunerative, the lessors will be forced to seek ways to increase the yield by other means. Older dwellings may be demolished or sold off to the occupants. The effect of this is a loss of older, cheaper dwellings. A measure to counteract such a trend is the system introduced in many countries whereby a permit must be sought for any change of use or demolition of a dwelling.

State intervention in rent prices may take place when a rent contract is concluded and may also cover any rent-price adjustments during the term of the contract. A special case is the ruling which covers the situation when an owner makes improvements. In most western ECE countries, rent prices are adjusted annually to bring them in line with the development of costs. This adjustment has usually already been agreed upon in the contract between tenant and lessor. The legislative authority often establishes rules on the procedure to be followed in such a case as well as the allowable amount of any rent-price increase. In the countries of eastern Europe, rent-price adjustments are less subject to market forces and more affected by political decisions. Rent-price increases occur when public financial conditions so warrant.

With regard to dwelling improvement, it is customary to counterbalance an increase in housing quality with an increase in rent price. To this end, the Government may prescribe the procedures to be followed and even fix the rent-price increase if the parties have not come to an agreement among themselves. Even in cases where the tenant benefits from a subsidy, it is generally considered appropriate that the Government should propose or determine the amount of the rent increase allowed.

## Chapter 2

## THE HOUSING STOCK AND DWELLING PRODUCTION

### I. PRELIMINARY REMARKS

This chapter outlines ways in which building initiatives are directed towards the creation of housing in the rental as opposed to the owner-occupied sector. Understanding this mechanism is central to the question of steering the desired composition of the housing stock. The last section presents country-by-country information on the housing stock and dwelling production.

Governments have the greatest influence on the rental sector when an important part of this sector is controlled by the public authorities or has been built under their aegis. If housing policy aims to encourage private investment in the rental housing sector, any measures that would dampen returns should, of course, be carefully watched. Governments influence housing-stock composition through rent-price policy.

Following the Second World War, the highest priority in most European countries was accorded to solving the housing shortage problem. In many countries, housing had been severely ravaged by war damage. The housing shortage was further compounded by demographic growth. Great efforts were made by public authorities and ordinary citizens to try to meet housing needs through new construction. Rental dwellings, in particular, were erected because most people in that era could not afford to buy housing. The subsidized rental sector also offered an appropriate means for realizing other social welfare objectives, such as building production continuity.

Dwelling production began to level off in western Europe around the mid-1970s. The most acute housing shortages had by then disappeared. There was an economic recession. Rising interest rates also had a restraining effect.

In the countries of eastern Europe, market developments were less influential. Czechoslovakia, the German Democratic Republic and the Soviet Union, for instance, continued building cheap rental units at a fast rate. In other countries of eastern Europe, the co-operative sector grew in importance alongside the rental sector with respect to dwelling production, while the share of owner-occupied housing decreased.

Once the crisis of housing quantity had abated, attention began to shift towards quality considerations. A great deal of the housing stock did not meet new requirements with regard to sanitation, lighting and heating. Moreover, as wages rose, demand for better-quality, more expensive housing also increased (for example, demand for single-family houses).

A policy oriented towards improvement of the housing stock may take as a basic assumption the likelihood

that owner-occupants will probably take greater care of their dwelling than a tenant-occupant. However, while they are usually quicker to make improvements to their housing, owner-occupants with very low incomes cannot afford substantial improvements.

In some countries, a large part of the old housing stock in the large cities is owned privately by people who have very little disposable income. Public authorities may need to pay increasing attention to this housing segment and allocate subsidies for home improvements, although this may be at the expense of the new construction of rental dwellings. There is ample evidence in any case that the production of dwellings in the rental sector has slowed down.

#### Initiatives and rental sector size

In the centrally-planned economies, private enterprise plays a minor role. It is the State that decides how much to invest in housing. It is also the State that sets the conditions by which investments are made.

In the market-economy countries, private enterprise leaves fairly wide scope for commercial initiative. Entrepreneurs invest in the construction of rental dwellings if there is a reasonable expectation of earning some return through rental income. When the rent price is lower than the running costs for the housing stock, new construction is not worth while from the financial viewpoint, unless a shortage is anticipated. Price regulation or restrictions on returns from rental income can thus inhibit investment in rental housing and serve as a brake to new construction in this sector. As a means to overcome this tendency, object subsidies may be proposed. They allow the rent price paid by tenants to remain below the cost-covering price structure, or more in line with average rent prices.

#### Demand side

For many tenants, rent price is a factor of prime importance when it comes to the questions of whether to purchase or rent a dwelling. People with low incomes are not faced with this choice, but if they are competing on the housing market for a rental dwelling, the rent price may well strain their limited budget. Consequently, the level of the rent price has considerable bearing on their housing consumption and satisfaction of space requirements.

Rent-price levels also have relevance to rental-dwelling demand. This is so partly because lower prices may allow young adults to move away from the parental dwelling at an earlier stage. If rent prices are high in relation to income, there will be a tendency to defer taking such a step.

In all the western ECE countries, Governments make some form of financial aid available for the housing of low-income groups, often beyond subsidization and fiscal measures covering the entire rental and owner-occupied sectors. Several countries have dwelling distribution systems intended to make cheaper dwellings available for low-income groups.

Affordability is usually an important issue for tenants in their choice of dwelling. The rent price which they will be required to pay limits the range of dwellings at their disposal. For the tenant, paying rent is a clear expense, whereas for owner-occupants the housing burden may to some extent be regarded as partly an investment or as savings.

In market-economy countries the choice of housing widens—both in terms of quality and quantity—the higher the rent price. This in turn means the higher the household income, the greater the choice of housing—the greater the variety of rental dwellings available. In the most expensive range, the supply is normally such that, in general, everyone with adequate means can occupy a dwelling of his or her own choosing. It is the house-hunter that determines the financial commitment and hence the qualitative and quantitative features of the housing selected. Excluded from this choice is that part of the housing stock reserved for those with low incomes. Consequently, people with high incomes will not readily find cheap, lower-quality dwellings.

For people with low incomes, their selection range is more restricted as they are seeking housing in a market sector where the supply is usually small and the demand great. They are often faced with lengthy waiting periods before appropriate accommodation becomes available. This situation varies considerably from one country to another, and also depends on rent prices in the housing stock as well as income distribution patterns.

Lower-income groups are housed almost entirely in the rental sector, the main exception being agrarian workers who may be supplied with cheap private housing. Low-income rural populations may inhabit owner-occupied dwellings that they have built themselves. As a result of increasing industrialization and urbanization, these groups will probably shift gradually towards the rental sector.

The question may arise why the housing of low-income groups is disproportionately represented in the rental sector, notwithstanding the far-reaching assistance schemes and favourable loan conditions often offered in many countries to promote owner-occupation. Some countries have recorded success with such incentives. The answer lies overwhelmingly in the fact that a low income does not offer any possibility to amass savings.

Housing acquisition may sometimes be considered a form of saving. However, even saving up a down payment may often be beyond the reach of certain income groups. Furthermore, those with low incomes may be in less secure positions in the labour market. Unskilled workers may be subject to unemployment and tend to find jobs at a slower rate than better-paid, more highly qualified workers. This uncertainty leads to a rather pru-

dent attitude towards an expensive purchase commitment.

Low incomes are proportionately higher in certain demographic groups such as older retired people and young single adults. The former cannot easily conclude a mortgage contract and the latter, because of their youth, often have no clear picture of the future or of their likely capabilities for making the commitment implied by a mortgage redemption spread over many years. Lastly, there are single people and single-parent households whose financial position is far from rosy. Such population groups often lack the financial means to buy a dwelling. The trend curves suggest that this group will continue to grow in many countries. So far, for those with limited financial means, the rental housing sector remains the most significant form of housing. Support to this group is one of the fundamental principles of rent policy in ECE countries.

## II. WESTERN EUROPE

### Austria

*Situation in 1982:*

Number of inhabitants per dwelling: 2.8
Housing stock: 2.66 million units
Population: 7.5 million

Rental dwellings, mainly multifamily houses, constitute 46 per cent of the housing stock; some 300,000 rental dwellings (24 per cent) have been built with public subsidies. Most of the dwellings are let through non-profit housing organizations; these vary in size. The largest organization runs a few thousand rental units. In Austria there is no clear-cut distinction between profit and non-profit lessors. Lessors may benefit from subsidies as long as they let a dwelling to a householder whose income is under a fixed limit. The nine provinces have established the criteria to be met by both lessor and tenant. The owner-occupied housing sector comprises mainly one-family houses. The focus is shifting away from new construction towards home-improvement. Subsidies for maintenance and renovation of the housing stock are increasing in size, particularly in the larger cities.

FIGURE 1

Dwelling production in Austria from 1973 to 1984

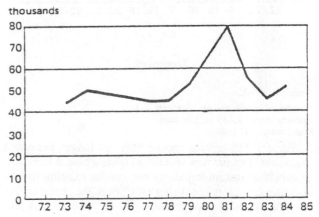

# Belgium

*Situation in 1981:*

Number of inhabitants per dwelling: 2.5
Housing stock: 3.948 million units
Population: 9.9 million

The 250,000 social rental dwelling units are mainly managed and operated by local housing societies which have often built both rental and owner-occupied dwellings.

Quantitatively, there is no shortage of housing. Dwelling production is consequently relatively low. During the period from 1971 to 1977, around 68 per cent of newly built dwellings were owner-occupied. About half of the new construction has been realized with public aid. The Government is now giving more and more emphasis to home-improvement.

FIGURE 2 a

**Composition of the housing stock in Belgium in 1980**

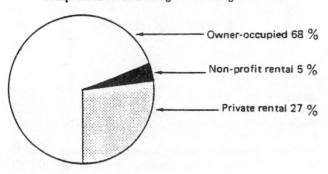

Owner-occupied 68 %

Non-profit rental 5 %

Private rental 27 %

FIGURE 2 b

**Dwelling production in Belgium from 1972 to 1985**

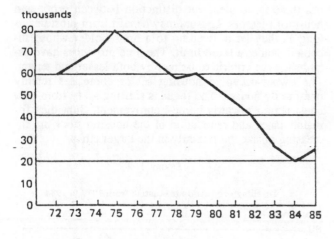

# Denmark

*Situation in 1982:*

Number of inhabitants per dwelling: 2.3
Housing stock: 2.133 million units
Population: 5.11 million

Since 1950, private lessors have no longer benefited from subsidies for new dwelling construction. Moreover, as subsidies to municipalities run out for existing dwellings, the emphasis is shifting away from the rental sector towards housing associations. Those associations are usually small (67 per cent manage fewer than 500 dwellings while only one manages more than 1,000 units).

The low level of new production accounts for the drop in the percentage of social rental housing. Between 1978 and 1982, the share of rental dwellings in new production averaged 29 per cent. Prior to 1975, new-dwelling production in Denmark was at a high level. Since the low point in 1982, dwelling production has edged up somewhat.

FIGURE 3 a

**Composition of the housing stock in Denmark in 1980**

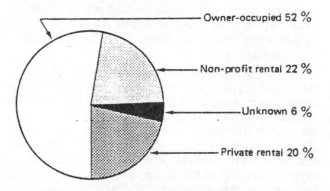

Owner-occupied 52 %

Non-profit rental 22 %

Unknown 6 %

Private rental 20 %

FIGURE 3 b

**Dwelling production in Denmark from 1972 to 1984**

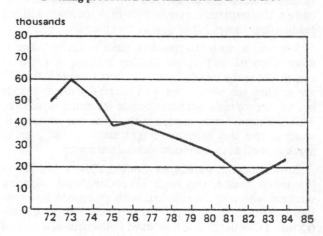

# Finland

*Situation in 1985:*

Number of inhabitants per dwelling: 2.56
Housing stock: 2.02 million units
Population: 4.86 million

Rental dwellings are generally owned by the local authorities, non-profit organizations, enterprises or private investors. Trade unions and student organizations are also actively engaged in the letting of dwellings. A quarter of the rental dwellings are linked to employment contracts.

Owing to the low rent returns, letting is not deemed commercially attractive. The share of rental dwellings in the housing stock has constantly decreased since 1950.

During the period from 1970 to 1985, the annual production of subsidized dwellings slowed from 21,500 to

18,800. Despite the lower rate of production, in 1985 some 10.2 dwellings per 1,000 inhabitants were completed.

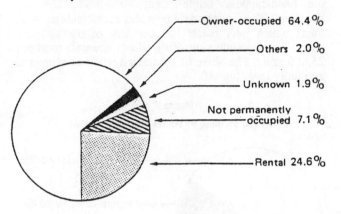

FIGURE 4 a

**Composition of the housing stock in Finland in 1985**

Owner-occupied 64.4%

Others 2.0%

Unknown 1.9%

Not permanently occupied 7.1%

Rental 24.6%

FIGURE 4 b

**Dwelling production in Finland from 1972 to 1985**

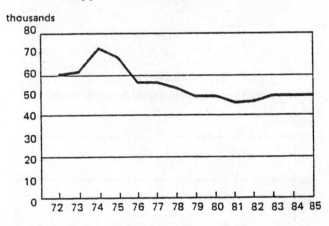

France

*Situation in 1982:*

Number of inhabitants per dwelling: 2.4
Housing stock: 22.7 million units
Population: 54 million

Three sectors constitute the rental housing stock: subsidized, regulated private, and free. Subsidized rental dwellings are run as HLMs (*Habitations à loyer moderé* or moderate rent dwellings) by non-profit associations. HLM dwellings are not exclusively for lower-income groups: less than half the active population with the lowest income is lodged in this category of housing.

In the private sector, it is necessary to distinguish between rental dwellings which are subject to the 1948 Act and those which are not. Rental dwellings built before 1948 and located in one of 3,000 municipalities are subject to the Act. The rent-price calculation and the yearly adjustments are determined by legislation. Rents in this category are relatively low. The second category comes under another régime within which (since 1 January 1987) rents are freely negotiated. Nearly 15 per cent

of private rental dwellings are built with the help of a loan subsidized by the State.

In 1981, new dwellings completed numbered 6.8 per 1,000 inhabitants. Construction by private lessors is now quite rare. In the period from 1972 to 1975, the private sector added around 50,000 dwellings per annum to the housing stock.

FIGURE 5 a

**Composition of the housing stock in France in 1980**

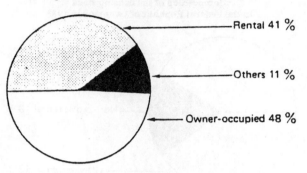

Rental 41 %

Others 11 %

Owner-occupied 48 %

FIGURE 5 b

**Dwelling production in France from 1972 to 1981**

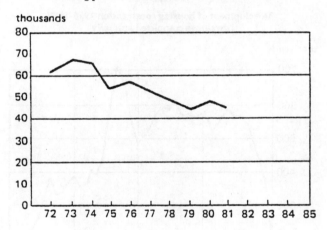

Federal Republic of Germany

*Situation in 1987 (Census of Population and Housing):*

Number of inhabitants per dwelling: 2.3
Housing stock: 26.2 million units
Population: 61.08 million

The annual housing output in the Federal Republic of Germany was high during the post-war period as a result of the housing shortage caused by destruction during the Second World War. An average of 10 dwellings per 1,000 inhabitants were completed each year in the 1950s and 1960s. With the reduction of the backlog demand during the post-war period, housing construction decreased. At present, the medium-term average is in the region of five dwellings per 1,000 inhabitants per annum.

The proportion of dwellings enjoying direct assistance in the publicly-assisted housing sector is around 20 per cent. In addition to this, indirect promotion via income tax also plays an important role in the construction of owner-occupied dwellings. While it is true that, in contrast with many other countries, interest on debt is not deductible from income tax, the purchase or production costs of an owner-occupied dwelling can be deducted from the income-tax base up to certain amounts for a period of eight years. Further assistance is provided for families with children.

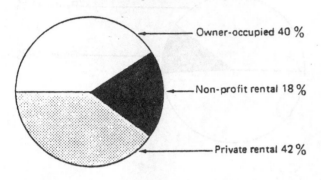

FIGURE 6 a

**Composition of the housing stock in the Federal Republic of Germany in 1985**

— Owner-occupied 40 %

— Non-profit rental 18 %

— Private rental 42 %

FIGURE 6 b

**Development of housing construction 1950-1988 dwellings completed annually**

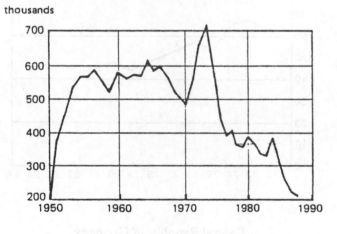

thousands

### Ireland

*Situation in 1981:*

Number of inhabitants per dwelling: 3.9
Housing stock: 0.894 million units
Population: 3.5 million

A considerable part of private rental dwellings is formed by those let furnished. For these no rent-price restrictions apply; this is not the case for unfurnished dwellings. Since 1946, the number of unfurnished rental dwellings has decreased by around 130,000 units. Dwellings in the special category mainly consist of those let within the framework of an employment contract. Subsidized rental dwellings (half the stock) have a rent price that is related to income. They are intended for habitation by people who cannot afford to bear the entire cost of shelter. Municipalities are actively engaged in the

housing field. More than a quarter of rental dwellings have been built by local authorities. About 170,000 units were sold to tenants over the years. There has therefore been an increase in owner-occupied housing. Local authorities increasingly devote themselves to housing construction for population categories like the elderly, the handicapped, single-parent households and the homeless. The Government provides municipalities with loans which may reach 100 per cent of the building costs. Yearly production of dwellings amounts to about 25,000 units. The share of subsidized rental dwellings is gradually levelling off.

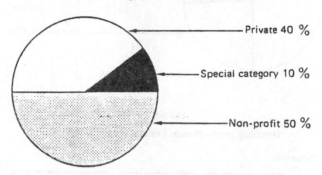

FIGURE 7 a

**Rental dwelling by tenure in Ireland in 1981**

— Private 40 %

— Special category 10 %

— Non-profit 50 %

FIGURE 7 b

**Dwelling production in Ireland from 1980 to 1985**

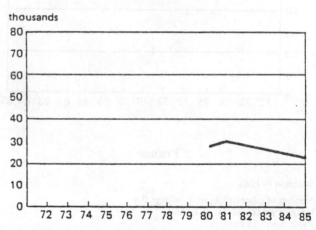

thousands

### Netherlands

*Situation in 1985:*

Number of inhabitants per dwelling: 2.7
Housing stock: 5.7 million units
Population: 14.5 million

On average, 57 per cent of the housing stock consists of rental dwellings, but in the larger cities the proportion often exceeds 80 per cent.

Until 1988, housing "corporations", registered with the government authorities, were eligible for State loans and extra subsidies. They were obliged to undergo strict controls of their financial management and rent-price policies. The 890 corporations (private, non-profit asso-

ciations) were established for the most part at the beginning of the century by trade unions, churches and social institutions. Their size varies. About 25 per cent own fewer than 600 dwellings while 12 per cent run more than 4,000. "Corporation" housing is intended for both lower- and middle-income groups. The number of municipal housing agencies is gradually diminishing; they amounted to around 330 in 1984. With regard to new construction, corporations take precedence over municipal agencies by law.

There are two groups of private investors. The largest proportion consists of investors (in particular insurance companies and pension funds) which let high-quality, expensive dwellings for the most part. The second (smaller) group consists of private individuals who let dwellings of a relatively moderate quality. Investors let 20 per cent of the rental stock.

During the period from 1975 to 1985, around 40 per cent of the construction of owner-occupied dwellings was completed without State aid. The share of rental dwellings in new construction decreased steeply during the 1970s. This trend has continued, but more gradually. It is expected that the share of owner-occupied housing will continue to increase.

## Norway

*Situation in 1983:*

Number of inhabitants per dwelling: 3.2
Housing stock: 1.524 million units (1980)

For many years, the housing policy has concentrated on owner-occupied housing. Condominium dwellings are now gaining impetus. This system now forms the core of the non-profit housing sector. Co-operative ownership (a stock of good, cheap dwellings) is transferable to others at a price strongly influenced by the local authorities.

Seventy-five per cent of the 381,000 rental dwellings are owned by private individuals. The 95,000 rental dwellings in the social housing sector are run by public authorities or co-operatives for pensioners, the handicapped or other special groups.

On account of the favourable financial conditions offered by the State Housing Bank during the 1970s, dwelling production reached a rate of over 10 per 1,000 inhabitants. While some 75 per cent of new construction benefited from this form of financing in the period from 1976 to 1980, in 1983 the percentage was 53.

FIGURE 8 a

**Composition of the housing stock in the Netherlands in 1985**

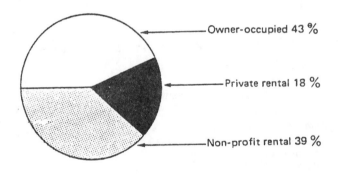

Owner-occupied 43 %

Private rental 18 %

Non-profit rental 39 %

FIGURE 9 a

**Composition of the housing stock in Norway in 1980**

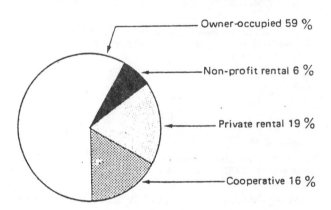

Owner-occupied 59 %

Non-profit rental 6 %

Private rental 19 %

Cooperative 16 %

FIGURE 8 b

**Dwelling production in the Netherlands from 1972 to 1986**

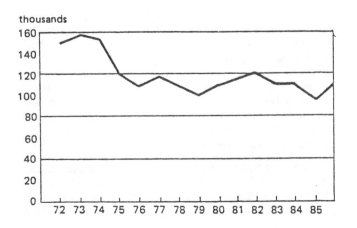

FIGURE 9 b

**Dwelling production in Norway from 1972 to 1981**

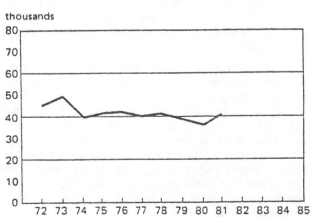

## Portugal

*Situation in 1981:*

Number of inhabitants per dwelling: 3.8
Housing stock: 2.653 million units
Population: 10 million

Around 100,000 dwellings are unoccupied because of their state of maintenance. During the 1970s, the number of rental dwellings declined. The Government tries to stimulate the rental sector by providing investors with subsidies and fiscal incentives. The rent price for most dwellings has been frozen for many years, but may be raised when a new lease contract is negotiated and rent prices are freed. In the case of dwelling renovation, a considerable increase in rent price may be made.

FIGURE 10

Composition of the housing stock in Portugal in 1981[a]

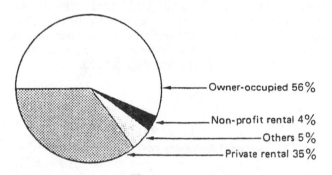

[a] Excludes vacant dwellings, holiday cottages and slums. Dwellings in co-operative ownership are considered owner-occupied.

FIGURE 11 a

Composition of the housing stock in Spain in 1981

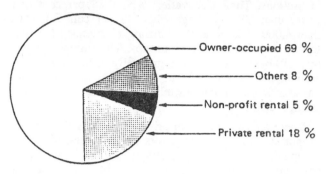

FIGURE 11 b

Dwelling production in Spain from 1972 to 1984

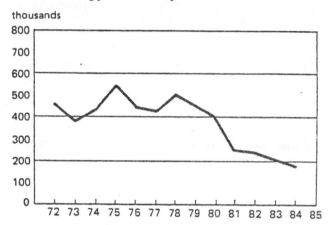

## Spain

*Situation in 1981:*

Number of inhabitants per dwelling: 2.6
Housing stock: 14.726 million units
Population: 38.3 million

Approximately 23 per cent of the stock is estimated to be in a bad state of maintenance. However, the quantitative supply of dwellings is more than sufficient. There is more than the 4 per cent vacancy rate required for a good functioning of the housing market. On average, 190,000 dwellings are unoccupied for a long period of time.

The increase in the number of secondary residences has contributed to an increase in the housing stock. In 1981, one in six households had a secondary residence at their disposal.

In the provincial capitals and in cities with over 100,000 inhabitants, the rental sector covers 35 per cent of the housing stock. In rural areas, the figure is 15 per cent. The share of the rental sector in the total housing stock had decreased from 50 per cent in 1950 to 23 per cent in 1980. The Government is endeavouring to stop this decrease. Rental dwellings are considered important because they demand lower expenditure by consumers and they allow greater population mobility. The objective is a 50:50 split between rental and owner-occupied housing.

## Sweden

*Situation in 1983:*

Number of inhabitants per dwelling: 2.3
Housing stock: 3.67 million units
Population: 8.33 million

The share of private rental dwellings dropped from 75 per cent in 1960 to under 50 per cent by 1980. This sector consists mainly of older apartment housing units occupied by elderly, one-person households. The share of municipal housing has increased sharply. Municipalities build multifamily housing in particular. This type of housing covers 73 per cent of the rental sector.

Since 1966, co-operatives have been recognized and financially aided by the Government. There are 155,000 co-operative dwellings of which 68,000 are rental. Until the mid-1970s, only existing rental dwellings could be converted into co-operatives. Later, only dwelling units in newly built estates qualified for co-operative ownership. Ninety-five per cent of the dwellings in the housing associations system were built after 1940; 60 per cent after 1960. Private rental dwellings are concentrated in the pre-war housing stock (75 per cent).

Owner-occupied housing is a sector that is growing as a result of the increasing demand for one-family houses. The policy is not to favour this sector over others. The Government endeavours to equalize the housing burden in the various sectors so that price disparities reflect only differences in quality.

Annual housing production in 1981 was 6.2 dwellings per 1,000 inhabitants. The share of the rental sector is shrinking.

New construction for the period from 1975 to 1980:

|  | *per cent* |
|---|---|
| Owner-occupied ........................................................ | 63 |
| Co-operatives ........................................................... | 10 |
| Rental: |  |
|    Municipal ........................................................ | 21 |
|    Private [a] ........................................................ | 4 |

[a] Ninety per cent have been built with the help of State loans.

FIGURE 13

Dwelling production in Sweden from 1972 to 1981

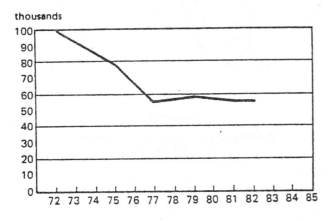

FIGURE 14 a

Composition of the housing stock in Switzerland in 1980

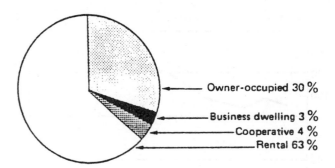

Owner-occupied 30 %

Business dwelling 3 %

Cooperative 4 %

Rental 63 %

FIGURE 14 b

Dwelling production in Switzerland from 1972 to 1983

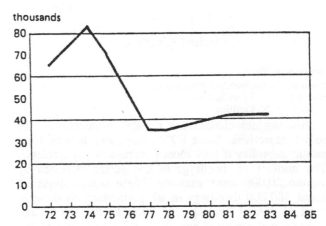

## Switzerland

*Situation in 1980:*

Number of inhabitants per dwelling: 2.6
Housing stock: 2.722 million units
Population: 6.4 million

There is a rather small public or semi-public rental sector. Most private lessors operate with a view to profit from rent returns. This form of investment is therefore in competition with other investment possibilities. Despite the high standard of living, there is a relatively low rate of owner-occupation. Possible reasons for this may include:

(*a*) A propensity to invest in areas other than housing because of the liberal rent-price system;

(*b*) High land prices put home ownership beyond the reach of many. The average price of a dwelling amounted to six to eight times the average annual income in 1981;

(*c*) The absence of stimulating subsidies and fiscal incentives.

Dwelling production during the 1980s was 7 per 1,000 inhabitants. The share of subsidized dwellings is low in comparison with other European countries.

## Turkey

*Situation in 1980:*

Number of inhabitants per dwelling: 5.2
Housing stock: 8.601 million units
Population: 45 million

The production of 120,000 dwellings means 2.6 per 1,000 inhabitants. A considerable part of the production is carried out through self-help.

FIGURE 15 a

Housing stock in 40 municipalities in Turkey with more than 10,000 inhabitants in the period 1978/1979

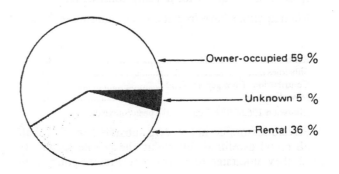

Owner-occupied 59 %

Unknown 5 %

Rental 36 %

FIGURE 15 b

Dwelling production in Turkey from 1972 to 1981

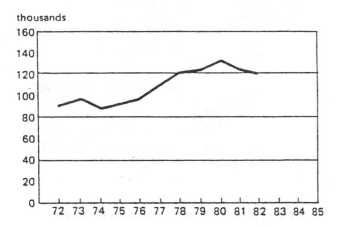

thousands

## United Kingdom

*Situation in 1982:*

Number of inhabitants per dwelling: 3.9
Housing stock: 22 million units
Population: 56.4 million

Housing associations are private organizations with social objectives. Since 1974, they may benefit from public subsidies if they meet government requirements. The number of dwellings in this sector increases by around 20,000 units annually. These organizations let about 580,000 dwellings in all, particularly to those in need of special housing (for example, the elderly and handicapped persons) and those whose income makes them ineligible for council houses.

The number of council houses has decreased by 1 million since 1979, mainly as a result of units being sold to tenants. In 1980, tenants acquired the right to purchase their council houses. Tenants who could not qualify for a mortgage loan on the open market were offered loans by the public authorities. Tenants who had inhabited their houses for a long time were eligible for a discount on the market price. Government policy continues to encourage owner-occupation.

Municipalities must balance revenue with expenses. The cut in subsidy contributions has obliged municipalities to increase rent prices. It is the lower-income group especially that is lodged in council housing.

For the construction of rental dwellings, municipalities must rely on funds borrowed on the capital market. The Government fixes the maximum amount that municipalities may borrow for housing construction.

Municipalities have four sources of housing revenue:

|  | per cent |
|---|---|
| Rents | 66 |
| Subsidies | 8 |
| Contributions from general fund | 10 |
| Miscellaneous | 15 |

(Situation 1983/1984; figures have been rounded.)

Private lessors do not receive subsidies. In 1951, half of all rental dwellings fell within the private sector. By 1982, they amounted to 12 per cent. Present policy is to stimulate private letting and enhance investments in the private rental sector:

| *Private letting* | *per cent* |
|---|---|
| Individuals | 60 |
| Investment funds | 10 |
| Employers | 30 |

FIGURE 12 a

Composition of the housing stock
in the United Kingdom in 1982

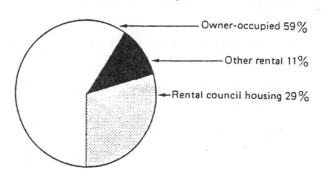

FIGURE 12 b

Dwelling production in the United Kingdom
from 1972 to 1982

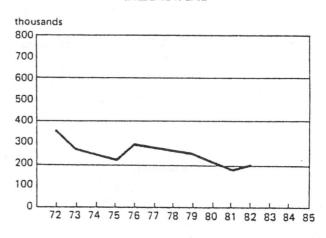

thousands

## III. EASTERN EUROPE

### Bulgaria

*Situation in 1985:*

Number of inhabitants per dwelling: 2.3
Housing stock: 3.9 million units
Population: 8.8 million

The majority of dwellings are in private ownership. More than 77 per cent of housing is owner-occupied; 21 per cent are rental units while 2 per cent are occupied by both owners and tenants.

Municipal authorities act as lessors for emergency housing supply in particular. Public bodies and enterprises let housing to their employees. Private entities may also act as lessors, provided the rent returns do not constitute a source of subsistence.

Every citizen may possess, in addition to a dwelling, a recreation house. The stimulation of owner-occupied housing by the authorities is shown by the fact that tenants have the possibility of buying their dwellings under certain conditions. To this end, a number of payment facilities have been introduced.

The share of rental dwellings increased, however, from 16 per cent in 1975 to 22 per cent in 1985. In the new construction programme, the level of rental dwelling construction is more or less equal to that of owner-occupied housing.

## Czechoslovakia

*Situation in 1980:*

Number of inhabitants per dwelling: 2.8
Housing stock: 5.37 million units
Population: 15.3 million

Rental dwellings are mainly run by State institutions and enterprises. The State fully subsidizes the construction and renovation of rental dwellings. The construction of co-operative and owner-occupied dwellings is aided by public subsidies and cheap loans.

Average dwelling production from 1976 to 1980: 130,000 units per annum, of which:

|                      | per cent |
| -------------------- | -------- |
| Public authorities   | 41       |
| Co-operative sector  | 30       |
| Owner-occupied       | 29       |

Average dwelling production from 1981 to 1983: 100,000 units per annum, of which:

|                      | per cent |
| -------------------- | -------- |
| Public authorities   | 18       |
| Co-operative sector  | 49       |
| Owner-occupied       | 33       |

FIGURE 16

Composition of the housing stock in Czechoslovakia in 1980

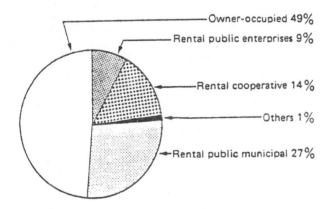

## German Democratic Republic

*Situation in 1981:*

Number of inhabitants per dwelling: 2.5
Housing stock: 6.562 million units
Population: 16.7 million

The majority of the stock consists of urban, multifamily housing. Private rental dwellings date back to pre-

1945 construction. The owner-occupied sector, including farmhouses, constitutes around 2 million dwellings, usually one- or two-family houses.

During the period from 1971 to 1983, an annual average of 101,000 dwellings were added to the housing stock, that is, some 6.5 units per 1,000 inhabitants. In that same period, an average of over 50,000 dwellings were renovated or modernized. Around 48 per cent of new construction belongs to the public sector; 42 per cent to co-operatives. More than 10 per cent of new construction consists of one-family houses.

FIGURE 17

Composition of the housing stock in the German Democratic Republic in 1981

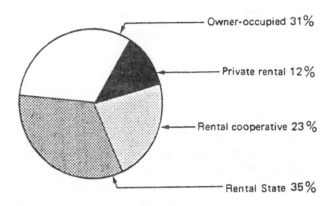

## Hungary

*Situation in 1980:*

Number of inhabitants per dwelling: 3
Housing stock: 3.542 million units
Population: 10.709 million

Owner-occupied dwellings amount to 73 per cent. The relatively small rental sector is by and large public.

Subsidized dwellings (in particular urban, multifamily housing) are primarily earmarked for lower-income households. There are income criteria for qualifying for housing in this sector, although an increase in income does not necessarily lead to departure.

Private rental dwellings are mostly located in part of owner-occupied houses. The construction of rental dwellings by private individuals is not permitted.

The Government stimulates home ownership (85 per cent of one-family houses) because owner-occupants are considered to take better care of their dwellings, with respect to maintenance and improvements, than tenants.

As there is no longer any significant housing shortage, attention is turning towards housing improvement. This policy is reflected in new dwelling-production figures. Dwelling production from 1976 to 1980 averaged 90,000 units per annum, of which more than 75 per cent of the newly built dwellings were intended to be occupied by their owners. Subsidies are granted for the acquisition or the construction of a home by means of self-help. Consequently, the percentage of owner-occupied dwellings continues to increase. Private individuals may

possess a recreation residence in addition to their primary residence.

FIGURE 18

Composition of the housing stock in Hungary in 1980

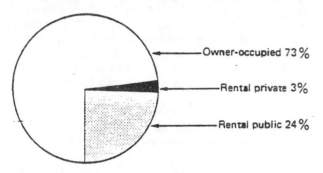

FIGURE 19

Composition of the housing stock in Poland in 1983

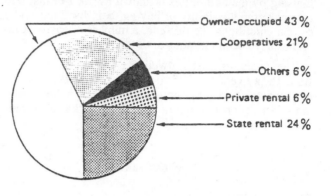

## Poland

*Situation in 1988:*

Number of inhabitants per dwelling: 3.5
Housing stock: 11.1 million units
Population: 37.8 million

The entire rental stock receives public financial aid. Dwellings are let on a non-profit basis.

Dwelling production by owner (percentage):

|                                        | 1960 | 1970 | 1978 | 1982 | 1983 | 1988 |
|----------------------------------------|------|------|------|------|------|------|
| Municipalities                         | 24   | 7    | —    | —    | 1    | 3    |
| Enterprises                            | 25   | 16   | 18   | 16   | 17   | 18   |
| Co-operatives                          | 10   | 49   | 56   | 55   | 53   | 45   |
| Private                                | 41   | 28   | 26   | 29   | 29   | 34   |
| Total dwelling production (in thousands) | 142  | 194  | 284  | 186  | 196  | 190  |

## Union of Soviet Socialist Republics

In 1982 some 72 per cent of dwellings were let by local authorities or State enterprises. There are relatively fewer co-operative dwellings than in some other countries of eastern Europe, although this sector is growing. For financial reasons, the State stimulates co-operative housing ownership. The occupants of co-operative dwellings pay more for their housing than a tenant does, although they can obtain loans at a low rate of interest. As income rises, an increase in the housing burden is not normally a problem.

The private sector is particularly significant in rural areas. Despite the lack of private dwelling construction in large cities, the owner-occupied housing sector comprises around 20 per cent of new dwelling production.

## Chapter 3

## RENT-PRICE POLICY AND DWELLING EXPLOITATION

### I. PRELIMINARY REMARKS

Theoretical points concerning rent policies were taken up in chapter 1, section III. This chapter covers actual rent-price regulation in the various ECE countries, starting with the question of how rent policies are attuned to the running costs of the lessor. A distinction is made between the public or social sector and the private rental sector. Another relevant distinction is that made between rent-price adjustments in the existing housing stock and the setting of rent prices for newly built dwellings or for new lease contracts. Section IV contains a recapitulation.

### II. WESTERN EUROPE

#### Austria

*Private rental sector*

These dwellings are covered by the 1981 Rent Act. Their rent price may not exceed certain limits, expressed in schillings per square metre of useful floor space. The maximum rent depends on the surface area and the technical equipment of the dwelling. Maximum rent prices are related to the consumer price index.

A rent-price increase is possible only if the lease contract contains an indexation clause. Rent-price adjustments are related to changes in the consumer price index. As to the current costs, the lessor can charge the tenant an amount equal to the actual cost or an estimated amount thereof. The indemnity for current costs may be increased by only 10 per cent annually.

*Social rental sector*

The principle of cost-price rent prevails. The following elements are considered: the net rent price (composed of capital charges, percentages of the cost of land and development, maintenance reserves, deduction of subsidies to the tenant), current expenditures, extraordinary expenses and services provided.

The sum of these components of the rent price is subject to 8 per cent VAT (value-added tax). The net rent is increased in line with the consumer price index. The indemnity covering current expenses can only be augmented if actual costs so dictate.

#### Belgium

*Private rental sector*

Rent prices in this sector are fixed upon transfer of the dwelling or when new lease contracts are negotiated between lessors and tenants. The rent does not have to be related to the amount of investment and interest charges. With tenants who remain longer than a year, the rent price may be adjusted annually. The increase may not exceed a percentage set by law (for the period from 1980 to 1983 it was fixed at 6 per cent). An expiring lease contract continues by law until the end of the current year. During such a continuation period, there can be no rent-price increase.

*Social rental sector*

Both the setting and adjustment of rent prices take place according to a system of basic rents and rebates using income coefficients. The basic rent is a percentage of the updated cost price of the dwelling. The income coefficient allows for moderation of the rent on the basis of the tenant's income. Thus the rents in the social sector are adjusted when a change occurs in the tenant's income, the standard income, the cost price of housing or living costs.

#### Denmark

*Private rental sector*

In those parts of the country where the housing stock is presumed to meet housing needs, the cost-price rent may be increased by a maximum of 8 per cent of the rental value of the dwelling. However, rent control applies to around 85 per cent of all rental dwellings. The cost-price rent is applicable to these dwellings. Rent increases are permitted only when total costs increase (the sum of capital charges, running costs and service costs).

*Social rental sector*

In this sector the cost-price rent applies. Rent increases are allowed when total costs rise; they may also be increased as a result of a lowering of interest subsidies.

#### Finland

*Private rental sector*

Within the framework of overall rent-price regulation, rent prices for newly built dwellings may be freely agreed upon. For rent-price adjustments, maximum annual amounts are established by the central Government. For higher rent increases, a court decision is required.

Maximum rent increases are based on the development of running costs. For this calculation, consideration is taken of management costs, interest rates and capital expenses.

*Social rental sector*

For newly built dwellings, a maximum per residential estate is calculated which fully covers the costs of construction, maintenance and capital expenses. The maximum rent per dwelling unit is derived from the average amount. The rent may be increased without approval by the authorities if it does not exceed the set limits. If higher rent is required, it has to be approved by the municipality. The rent price is usually set for one year, taking into consideration mortgage redemption, rate of interest, the cost of land and maintenance costs (according to a detailed calculation). Any surplus or deficit from the previous year is also taken into account. If the rent price surpasses a reasonable market level, the tenant may seek redress in court for a decrease in rent.

The system of reasonable market rents predominates over the cost-price system. Every year the Government issues directives as to the reasonable local market level, on the basis of rent price statistics. When determining the reasonable or fair rent price for a dwelling unit, account must be taken of the age and quality of the dwelling and residential environment surrounding it.

## France

*Private rental sector*

The rent price consists of both actual rent and rent charges. The rent is based on:

(a) Interest and mortgage redemption costs;

(b) A return on the capital invested;

(c) Major maintenance and repair costs;

(d) Management costs, taxes and other charges.

The rent charges are the servicing costs which the owner/lessor may recover from the tenant. They are fixed by a decree setting limits for expenses. In the case of the first lease contract, or when the dwelling is vacant for more than 18 months as a result of a verdict in court for non-fulfilment of a tenant's obligations, the lessor and potential tenant may agree on the amount of the rent price by free negotiation.

In the county commissions and national commission, collective lease agreements may be concluded. There are four rental sectors:

(a) HLM;

(b) Other social lessors;

(c) Institutional investors;

(d) Other private lessors.

Before 1 January of each year, the national commission may fix, for each of these four sectors, maximum rent adjustments upon the conclusion or renewal of lease contracts. This rent-price agreement may also determine

how far the rent price may deviate from that of comparable dwellings in the area. It may also cover arrangements as to any extra rent increase after dwelling renovation. The rent-price regulations may vary according to districts.

If no agreement is reached at the national level, the Government can fix the maximum rent-price increase after consultation with the national commission. The percentage increase must be in line with the building cost index for at least 80 per cent of the amount.

*Social rental sector*

The social rental sector also has the possibility of collective rent-price/lease agreements.

## Federal Republic of Germany

*Private rental sector*

The rent is fixed by negotiations between lessors and tenants. Negotiations also determine what is covered by the rent. Rent adjustments may be made annually, provided that the rent asked does not exceed that of comparable dwellings in the same district. The rent increase over three years cannot exceed 30 per cent. A second method of rent adjustment is one whereby the parties agree on a fixed percentage of annual increase in the rent. Such an agreement may cover a maximum period of 10 years.

*Publicly-assisted rental sector*

The rent reflects capital charges and running expenses. Expenses include investment costs, mortgage redemption, cost of administration, running costs, maintenance expenses and the risk of rent income losses. The cost-covering rent is the basic starting point. As the interest subsidies shrink in the course of time, the gap must be filled by a rent increase to cover capital charges. For the rest, rent increases are allowed only in the case of higher current expenses.

## Ireland

*Private rental sector*

This sector is composed of a free sector and one that is partly controlled. The former mainly consists of furnished housing in urban areas. For furnished dwellings there are no restrictions as to rent price or rent adjustments and there is no tenant protection against notice to vacate. In the partly controlled sector, rent-price adjustments are agreed upon by negotiation between tenants and lessors. However, failing such agreement, since August 1983 a Rent Tribunal fixes the rent price. The Tribunal takes into account the character and location of the dwelling, the stipulations in any agreement, the date and purchase price of the dwelling, the duration of the tenant's occupation, the size and composition of the tenant's household. Any improvements made by the tenant are also considered.

*Social rental sector*

The rent price of municipal dwellings is calculated as a percentage of the disposable income of the tenant. This percentage runs from 5 per cent for the lowest incomes to 14 or 15 per cent, although the rent price may not exceed 5.25 per cent of the construction costs (updated by corrections for inflation). The system is periodically readjusted. The amount of the object subsidy depends on the construction costs and the rent price asked.

## Netherlands

### Private rental sector

In the non-aided sector, lessor and tenant are, in principle, free to negotiate the rent price. In practice, however, one cannot agree on a rent price higher than a maximum rent level attuned to the quality of the dwelling. Rent-price increases have an annual maximum for the whole national rental stock (trend increases). This maximum is fixed every year on a national basis, taking into account:

(a) The harmonization of rent prices in the existing rental stock with those for newly built dwellings;

(b) Any changes in construction-cost redemption, any increase in running costs: the rent increase should cover the increase in costs;

(c) The impact on the purchasing power of the tenants; income development;

(d) The consequences for the Government with regard to financial obligations for both individualized subsidies and object subsidies.

The trend increase is the maximum percentage increase for dwellings that have a rent price in fair conformity with quality. Higher maximum prices apply to dwellings for which the rent price is too low in terms of quality. The quality of the dwelling is measured with the help of a quality point system: the dwelling evaluation system. The policy pursued aims at an overall harmonious rent-price pattern.

### Social rental sector

The initial rent price of State-aided dwellings is calculated at the very beginning of exploitation as a percentage of the construction costs. The rent-price adjustment for dwellings in the stock is, in principle, made along the same lines as for the private rental sector. However, the maximum rent-price increase is also the minimum to be applied. Consequently, social lessors—the so-called "corporations" and the municipal housing agencies—are obliged to harmonize rents.

The subsidies are related to dwelling quality while detailed prescriptions are issued on the rent level. In this way, commissioners of public housing are stimulated to optimize the quality:cost ratio.

## Norway

### Private rental sector

The rent price is fixed in negotiations between lessors and tenants. Changes in rent price are made by mutual agreement. With the exception of the three largest cities, no specific rent-price adjustment policy is pursued. The annual increase usually corresponds to the rate of inflation. Nevertheless, there are some protective measures against unfair rent-price demands or rent increases:

(a) It is forbidden to ask an unfair rent price (Price Act);

(b) According to the Rent-price Regulation Act, a maximum rent level can be determined;

(c) According to the Rent Act, the Court may reduce the rent price of a dwelling to a rent level that is fair in terms of the value of the dwelling.

### Social rental sector

Both the fixing of rent prices and the rent adjustment are arranged in the same way as in the private sector.

## Portugal

### Private rental sector

There is a distinction to be made between "free" rents and rents with "conditions" attached. The only restriction on free rents is that subsequent rent adjustments are not allowed. The rent-price level of controlled rents is related to the value of the dwelling, with annual rent increases made on the basis of a formula established by law. The parameters of the formula are published on 31 October of the preceding year. Elements which figure in the calculation are: surface area, average construction cost per square metre, age and average maintenance cost per square metre. The annual rent price is 7 per cent of the value, thus calculated. Any rent increase is 7 per cent of the difference between the calculated values of two consecutive years.

### Social rental sector

The technical rent price is determined with the help of a formula according to the cost of interest and mortgage redemption of the capital invested, maintenance and administrative expenditures. The social rent price is determined by considering the size of the dwelling and the economic situation of the tenant. The Government pays the difference between the technical and the social rent prices.

## Spain

### Private rental sector

A distinction must be made between subsidized and non-aided dwellings. Non-aided dwellings have no restrictions as to the rent level. For subsidized dwellings, the rent level may not exceed 6 per cent of construction costs.

Rent-price adjustments relate to the time when the lease agreement was concluded. In the case of rent contracts made before 1956, the rent prices are frozen. For contracts concluded between 1956 and 1964, only one single rent increase has taken place—in 1972—after which rents were frozen. For contracts signed after 1964, a rent-price increase is applied up to a maximum fixed by the Government, provided that the lease contract contains a rent-increase clause.

*Social rental sector*

Rent prices for public housing are fixed at 3 per cent of construction costs. For rent increases, the same system applies as described above.

## Sweden

*Private rental sector*

In principle, rent prices are negotiated freely between tenants' and lessors' organizations. The collective negotiations are regulated by the "Rent Negotiation Act". The rent price of a dwelling is fixed on the basis of its use-value. This value refers to equal dwellings in the same municipality. Dwellings owned by the municipality thus function as trend setters. For the determination of the rent prices, municipal lessors have prepared directives that operate as a dwelling evaluation system (see chapter 4). In principle, the rent-price adjustment follows along the same lines. Each year, negotiation rounds are held at the national level, and any rent increase recommended is determined for the agreements to be reached at the local level. The agreements in the public sector are used as guidelines for negotiations for the private sector.

*Social rental sector*

Rent prices are set and adjusted along the same lines as in the private rental sector.

## Switzerland

*Private rental sector*

With the exception of State-aided dwellings, there is no traditional rent-price control. Rents are freely negotiated. Rent-price adjustments are likewise free of control. There are however certain provisions against abuse in the rental sector (see chapter 6, section II—Switzerland).

*Social rental sector*

In the federal sector the initial rent price is fixed at 5.1 per cent of the investment costs, i.e. below the rent necessary to cover the initial costs. The difference between cost-price rent and the initial rent level is covered by public loans. Rents are increased every two years by 6 per cent up to the twelfth year, at which time the cost-covering level is reached. Subsequently, the rent increase is determined in such a way that the repayment of the loan is settled within 25 years.

## United Kingdom

*Private rental sector*

Lessors and tenants agree on the rent price. However, either party can ask a "rent officer" to determine a so-called "fair rent". The rent officer considers the size, age, location and state of maintenance of the dwelling. His judgement is based on the assumption that offer and demand are in equilibrium. The "fair rent" is the legal maximum rent price for the dwelling, thus examined. Once every two years, the rent officer may determine a new rent price. Meanwhile, no rent-price alteration is allowed, unless both tenant and lessor jointly submit an application or circumstances have changed significantly (e.g. major repairs or improvements have been made, or if there are changes in either party's obligations). The new rent price is determined by applying a staged rent increase fixed at two steps per year. In practice, this means that every year a rent-price adjustment takes place.

*Social rental sector*

Municipal housing managers are concerned with the following expense items: capital charges, maintenance costs and administrative expenditure. The revenue comes from government contributions and rents paid. According to legal prescriptions, the revenue may not be inferior to the expenses. Thus rent price depends on government contributions.

An important element of the rent-price policy is that the rents of "council houses" are equalized. Starting from the rent revenue needed to cover costs, the rent prices are calculated per dwelling with the help of a differentiation model which accounts for elements such as size, standard of equipment, location, etc.

Object subsidies are given in the form of a lump-sum contribution covering the unpaid remainder of the investment amount, taking into account a fair rent revenue. There are no subsidies for the construction of council housing. Unpaid gaps in the investment costs must, in principle, be financed by rent revenues from all municipal properties after deduction of government subsidies for running costs.

## III. EASTERN EUROPE

### Bulgaria

In the private rental sector, the rent-price level is negotiated between lessor and tenant. However, there is a maximum amount per square metre of useful floor space of 2 leva in the large cities, 1.6 leva in medium-sized cities, and 0.8 leva in villages. According to quality differences, the rent price may be corrected by minus 50 per cent to plus 20 per cent. The rent of State-owned dwellings is 0.18 leva per square metre of useful floor space. Corrections for quality differences may run from minus 50 per cent to plus 32 per cent. The basic rental income is not sufficient to cover all the maintenance expenses of the dwellings.

### Czechoslovakia

Rent prices are set at a firmly-fixed tariff per square metre of floor space. There are four tariffs for dwellings, varying according to quality levels. The rent price is not directly related to construction or running costs. Depending on the size of the household, a rebate on the rent price is applied.

## German Democratic Republic

Rents are kept extremely low. The rent price has no relation to construction/renovation costs or current expenses. A lessor is not allowed to ask a rent price other than the one which has been legally prescribed. In Berlin the rent price amounts to 1.0 to 1.25 marks per square metre of floor space; elsewhere in the country it stands at 0.8 to 0.9 marks per square metre. Rent-price differentiation is based on dwelling quality. The rent prices of dwellings built before the Second World War (private dwellings included) are frozen, although a quality distinction is applied even in this case. About one third of running costs are covered by the rent price.

## Hungary

In the public sector, rent prices are independent of investment costs. In addition to the rent, new tenants are obliged to pay a fee when taking over a dwelling. This fee, calculated according to the quality of the dwelling, is determined by the central administration, and amounts to 6 to 10 per cent of the capital charges. In the case of exchange of dwelling, any difference in the fees of the two dwellings must be made up. The municipalities can deduct or remit the amount that is payable. Rent prices are lower than current expenses, maintenance costs or the cost of periodic improvements; the differences are reimbursed from the State budget. In 1989, owing to increasing construction costs, the yearly rent price of newly built dwellings did not reach even 1 per cent of capital costs. Interest and capital repayment costs are not included in the rent prices. Rent prices in the private sector cannot exceed twice the amount of those in the public sector.

Since 1 January 1989, new rental contracts in the private sector may be concluded freely between lessor and tenant. In the case of unfairness, a party can apply to the civil court. In the public sector, the differentiation of rent prices depends on dwelling quality. Between 1 July 1983 and 1 July 1988, rent prices rose by 200 to 300 per cent, so that they might cover the current expenses (excluding capital costs). This target was not reached, on account of growing inflation in recent years.

## Poland

Regardless of the category of the lessor, the rent price is calculated according to a standard legal amount per square metre of floor space. The amount of the rent for a specific house, however, is determined by the dwelling's quality. From 1983 up to and including 1985, rent prices were increased to such an extent that, by and large, the maintenance costs (except major renovation expenses) could be covered by rent revenue. In 1983 approximately 22 per cent of the maintenance costs were covered by rent income.

Since 1983 an attempt has been made to modify the ratio of government and tenant contributions to the costs of maintenance of the rental stock. However, no results have been achieved so far.

Successive increases in rent prices have hardly made it possible to keep the tenant's contribution at the same level. This is mainly due to the high rate of inflation in Poland (the most recent rent adjustment took place in 1989).

In spite of attempts to have the maintenance costs (water supply, waste disposal, etc.) as well as minor repairs covered by rent, usually not even the maintenance costs are covered. It is worth mentioning that major renovation work is financed by the State in the form of subsidies. Altogether, 25 per cent of the maintenance costs of the rental stock (running costs plus capital improvements) are financed by the rent revenue.

Radical changes regarding rent policy are proposed within the framework of economic reform and are being systematically introduced. This should mean that maintenance and renovation costs are fully covered by tenants.

## IV. RECAPITULATION

This chapter took up the question of how and to what extent rent-price policy in the various ECE countries was attuned to the exploitation costs sustained by the owner/lessor. The methods of setting the rent price and of adjusting it have been described country by country. The following chart gives a brief outline of how costs are carried over into rent prices.

RECAPITULATION TABLE

Rent-price policy and dwelling exploitation

| Country | Rental sector | Rent-price setting | Rent-price adjustment | Relationship to costs |
|---|---|---|---|---|
| **Western Europe** | | | | |
| Austria ............... | Profit | Free negotiations + maximum | Consumers price index + increase of current expenses to maximum | No direct relation to setting rent price, except for adjustment |
| | Non-profit | Cost-price rent | *Idem* | Direct relation |
| Belgium ............... | Profit | Free negotiations | Free negotiations + maximum | No direct relation |
| | Non-profit | Rent price is percentage of updated cost price × income coefficient | Rent-price changes with changes in cost price or income | Direct relation |
| Denmark ............. | Profit | Cost-price rent or cost-price rent + 8 per cent | With variable overall costs | Direct relation |
| | Non-profit | Price asked is cost price minus rent subsidies | With variable overall costs | Direct relation |
| Finland ............... | Profit | Free negotiations | Maximum increase based on cost development; maximum fair market level | No direct relation but for adjustments |
| | Non-profit | Cost-price rent | Altering overall costs; maximum fair market level | Direct relation |
| France ................. | Profit | Free negotiations | Rent-increases maximum restricted in rent-price agreements | No direct relation |
| | Non-Profit | *Idem* | *Idem* | *Idem* |
| Germany, Federal Republic of ..... | Profit | Free negotiations | Maximum increase 30 per cent over three years; local comparisons | No direct relation |
| | Non-profit | Rent asked is cost price minus rent subsidies | Altering costs or lessening object subsidies | Direct relation |
| Ireland ................. | Profit | Free negotiations | Free negotiations | No direct relation |
| | Non-profit | Free negotiations or by "Rent Tribunal" | Free negotiations or by "Rent Tribunal" | No direct relation |
| Netherlands .......... | Profit | Non-aided: free negotiations, but with maximum | Free negotiations, but with maximum | No direct relation |
| | | Subsidized: rent asked is cost-price rent minus subsidy | Free negotiations, but with maximum | Direct relation when setting price but not for adjustments |
| | Non-profit | *Idem* | Trend increase percentage, based on cost development, etc. | More or less direct |
| Norway ............... | Profit | Free negotiations + maximum | Free negotiations + maximum | No direct relation |
| | Non-profit | *Idem* | *Idem* | *Idem* |
| Portugal ............... | Profit | Free negotiations | No rent adjustments | No direct relation |
| | | Controlled by law linked to dwelling value | Increase updated value + maintenance costs | Direct relation |
| | Non-profit | Rent asked is cost price minus rent subsidy | As income changes | Direct relation for setting price, not for adjustments |
| Spain ................... | Profit | Non-aided: free negotiations | Contracts before 1964: rent frozen; after 1964: free negotiations + maximum | No direct relation |
| | | Subsidized: free negotiations + maximum | *Idem* | *Idem* |
| | Non-profit | 3 per cent of construction costs | *Idem* | Direct relation for setting price, not for adjustments |
| Sweden ............... | Profit | Free (collective) negotiations, depending on use-value | Local administration; collective negotiations | No direct relation |
| | Non-profit | *Idem* | *Idem* | *Idem* |

| Country | Rental sector | Rent-price setting | Rent-price adjustment | Relationship to costs |
|---|---|---|---|---|
| Switzerland ............ | Profit | Free negotiations | Free negotiations + maximum | No direct relation |
| | Non-profit | Initial rent is cost-price rent minus subsidy | As subsidies decline | Direct relation |
| United Kingdom .... | Profit | Free negotiations + maximum of fair rents | New fair rent determined by the "rent officer" | No direct relation |
| | Non-profit | Municipal administration | When municipal budget changes | No direct relation |
| *Eastern Europe* | | | | |
| Bulgaria .................. | Private | Free  negotiations + maximum | Free negotiations + maximum | No direct relation |
| | Public | Standardized; quality differentiation | Altering standards | *Idem* |
| Czechoslovakia ....... | Private and public | Standardized + quality differentiation | Altering standards | No direct relation |
| German Democratic Republic ............ | Private and public | Standardized + quality differentiation | Altering standards | No direct relation |
| Hungary .................. | Private: rental contracts signed until 1989 | Free negotiations + maximum of 2 × rents in public sector | Modified average in public sector | No direct relation |
| | Private: new rental contracts signed since 1989 | Free negotiations (court decision in case of unfairness) | Modified average in public sector | Direct relation |
| | Public | Standardized | Altering standards | *Idem* |
| Poland ..................... | Private and public | Standardized + quality differentiation | Altering standards | No direct relation |

## Chapter 4

## RENT-PRICE POLICY AND DWELLING QUALITY

### I. PRELIMINARY REMARKS

A clear-cut connection between rent price and dwelling quality is relevant to flexibility in the housing market. Many ECE countries have a policy aimed at attuning rent price to dwelling quality: this is the so-called rent harmonization policy.

This chapter compares the ways in which the various ECE countries pursue this policy. It covers rent-price adjustments in the dwelling stock and the setting of rent prices for newly built dwellings (new lease contracts) as well as home improvement. The question of how to measure quality is also raised. A final section gives a recapitulation of the most relevant data.

### II. WESTERN EUROPE

#### Austria

Rental dwellings in the private sector are subject to the 1981 Rent Act. The rent price of these dwellings may not go beyond a certain limit, expressed in schillings per square metre of useful floor space. The maximum rent is fixed by the provinces and depends on the surface area of the dwelling and its technical equipment. There are four quality classes, namely:

(*a*) Dwellings without sanitary provisions or running water;

(*b*) Dwellings with a water supply and toilet;

(*c*) Dwellings with at least one room, a kitchen, private entry, toilet and bath facilities;

(*d*) Dwellings with at least one room, a kitchen, private entry, toilet and bath facilities, central heating and a hot-water supply.

For the last category, a maximum rent price has not existed since 1984. Maximum rents are increased or lowered according to the rise and fall of the consumer price index. As a rule, rent increases also follow the consumer price index. For non-profit dwellings, the principle of cost-price rents is generally applied. Here, there is no direct relation between rent price and dwelling quality.

#### Belgium

In the private rental sector, the rent level and rent increases are determined by negotiation between lessor and tenant. The ratio of rent price to dwelling quality is expressed by shifts in demand and supply relations. In the social rental sector, the rent price depends, among other factors, on investment costs. Quality is expressed in terms of investment costs.

#### Denmark

Rent-price policy aimed at aligning rent prices of older and newer dwellings was introduced in 1965. The reason for this was the diverging historical pattern of cost-price rent since building costs had escalated.

Rent equalization schemes were devised whereby the rent-price level of older stock would gradually be raised to bring it into line with that of new construction which would likewise be lowered, so that by the end of an eight-year period (1974), the rent-price policy could then be abandoned. However, on account of high interest rates, increasing production costs and a strong inflation rate, it was not possible to accomplish this task. Later, no endeavours were made to harmonize rents or phase out disparities. Rent price is now defined as cost-price rent in both the profit and non-profit sectors. There is no direct relation between rent price and dwelling quality.

#### Finland

In principle, rent price is calculated as the cost-price rent. However, when the amount exceeds a level that is fair in relation to the market situation, the tenant may appeal to the courts for a lower rent. The Government issues annual directives on a fair or reasonable local rent level, which is established according to statistics. Reasonable rent is determined on the basis of dwelling quality. Factors taken into consideration are the age of the dwelling, the number of rooms, the standard of amenities in the dwelling and building, the location of the dwelling in the building and in the city, any nuisance factors in the surroundings (noise, air pollution, etc).

#### France

On both the local and national levels, collective rent agreements are possible. This applies to both social and private lessors. Quality is taken into account in so far as the rent-price agreement can fix the maximum deviation of the rent price from the rent level of comparable dwellings in the same area. The agreement may also stipulate the amount of a rent increase in the case of home improvement.

32

## Federal Republic of Germany

The rent in the privately financed sector is, in principle, fixed by negotiation between lessor and tenant. However, the tenant is protected against unreasonable rent-price increases by a system of comparative rents. Rents can only be increased if the rent asked does not exceed the rent level of comparable dwellings in the same area. The lessor is obliged to present a verifiable statement of comparable dwellings and rent levels. It is normally compared with a survey of rent levels prepared by the local authorities or by lessors' or tenants' associations. In it, the rent is generally indicated and differentiated according to dwelling age, quality (number of baths, toilets, as well as type of heating system, etc.) and location. The lessor may also determine the comparable rent by submitting an expert's report or by making reference to three comparable dwellings. Over a period of three years, the rent may not be increased by more than 30 per cent even if in the process, the local comparable rent level is not reached.

If the owner of a dwelling carries out modernization work, the rent may be increased in one of two ways: (a) by virtue of the improved quality of the dwelling, a higher comparative rent applies. The rent can be adjusted to this following the procedure outlined above; (b) alternatively, the owner can transfer 11 per cent per annum of the expenditure on modernization work to the rent. Public grants must be deducted in calculating the relevant amount. Costs for simple repair and maintenance work may not be passed on to the tenant.

In the publicly-assisted rental sector, the cost-covering rent principle is applied. Rent increases are allowed only in so far as current expenses rise or property-related subsidies fall. There is no explicit relationship between rent and dwelling quality.

## Ireland

In the private rental sector, tenants and lessors may make an agreement on rent price, as desired. While quality may count, it is not set as a legal matter. In part of this sector, an independent body may fix the rent price in the absence of an agreement between the parties. This independent body takes into account the nature, characteristics and location of the dwelling concerned.

In the social rental sector, the rent price is based on the income of the tenant. The rules are periodically reviewed and adapted to cost development, inflation and the financial situation of the municipality, among other considerations. There is no express relation between rent price and dwelling quality.

## Netherlands

For new construction, subsidized and non-aided rental sectors have different rules for fixing the rent price. The rent price of subsidized new dwellings depends on the building costs (from which are deducted subsidies that depend on dwelling size). For the non-aided rental

dwellings, the rent price may not exceed the maximum in the relevant quality class.

Rent adjustments in the housing stock are made according to the rent-price increase trend which indicates the maximum percentage for dwellings; price corresponds reasonably well with quality. For dwellings for which the price is too low in relation to quality (below the fair minimum), higher maximum levels apply.

Dwelling quality is measured with the help of an objective housing evaluation system. The system gives points for each aspect of the dwelling; the most important criterion is the surface area of rooms (more than half of all the points for new constructions). Other criteria include heating, thermal insulation, kitchen equipment, sanitary installations, age, garden, type of dwelling, residential environment and nuisance factors. The minimum and maximum fair rents are determined per dwelling by multiplying the number of points with a minimum and a maximum fair price per point. The rent-price policy endeavours to match rents of newly built dwellings with those in the existing stock so that a uniform price/quality ratio is obtained for all dwellings.

## Norway

In principle, rent prices in both the private and the public rental sectors are set and adjusted in the same way. The rent price is agreed upon in negotiations between tenants and lessors. The ratio of rent price to quality is determined by the market situation. For the three largest cities, a special rent-price system prevails. The amount of rent is fixed according to criteria such as dwelling size, quality and location. Actual implementation shows many variations. In case of a dispute over the rent price, the reasonableness of the rent price is judged in court according to such criteria as the value of the dwelling and the number of rooms.

## Portugal

In the case of "free" rents in the private sector, there is no direct relation between rent price and quality; the market mechanism prevails. As for set rents, there is an established connection between the rent price and the value of the dwelling. This value is calculated according to a legal formula that pertains to quality, age and surface area of the dwelling. Rent-price adjustments are also calculated on the basis of this formula (increase of value).

In the public housing sector, the quality aspect is reflected in the rent differentiation system. Rent prices per dwelling are calculated using the differentiation system taking into account the required overall rent revenue of the municipality. In this system, elements such as size, type of equipment, etc., are taken into account.

## Spain

In the private rental sector a distinction is made between subsidized and non-aided dwellings. The rents of non-aided dwellings are, in principle, free of control. The level of rents of subsidized dwellings is fixed at 6 per cent of the construction costs.

In the social rental sector, the rent price amounts to 3 per cent of the construction costs. The quality aspect is expressed in the rent price only in so far as quality has a bearing on the amount of the construction costs. The rent (adjustment) policy has created a considerable difference among rent levels in the various contract periods.

## Sweden

In rent-price policy, quality plays an important role in both the social and the private rental sectors. The social rental sector functions as the trend setter. For fixing the rent price, municipal lessors use a dwelling evaluation system, which includes such factors as: year of construction, location, number of rooms, dwelling type, kitchen equipment, floor space, view, bathroom facilities, balconies, etc. Quality points are attributed to each dwelling according to these factors. These points are calculated per area, then multiplied by the number of points applied for setting the rent price in the particular area (location). At the next stage values are attributed for the entire property. The rent revenue determined by calculation is divided by the sum of points of the whole property of the lessor. The resulting amount is the rent price per quality point. On this basis the rent asked is determined per dwelling.

At the central level, annual negotiations take place between tenants' and lessors' organizations, and any recommended rent increase is fixed. Rent increases are determined by calculating the rent revenue needed for the next year; an allotment by individual dwelling is then made.

## Switzerland

In the private sector, quality does not in itself play a role in determining the level of the rent price or adjustments, except through the market mechanism. In case of a dispute, when checking the reasonableness of the rent price, the quality aspect is also examined. The examination is carried out by a special commission in which both parties are represented (rent commission).

Subsidies are granted in the social rental sector according to a very detailed model of quality, the so-called Wohnungs-Bewertungs-System (Housing Evaluation System). The system is, in practice, also used to indicate the quality of dwellings in negotiations on the rent price in the private sector. The relation between rent price and quality has not been set in legislation.

In the social rental sector, the level of the initial rent price depends on the construction costs. Rent increases are fixed in such a way as to enable the repayment of the costs within 25 years. There is no direct relation between rent price and quality other than that expressed in the quality aspects which figure in the construction costs.

## Turkey

The rent price is determined only through the market mechanism. When judging the reasonableness of the rent price in the case of disputes, the quality aspect comes to bear in terms of:

(a) Proximity to the city centre;

(b) Location (social status, rent level, surroundings);

(c) Standard of equipment;

(d) Size of dwelling.

## United Kingdom

In the private sector, the level of the rent price is determined by consultation between lessor and tenant. Either party can ask a "rent officer" to fix a "fair rent" which will be the legal maximum. In the decision, the rent officer takes into account size, location and state of maintenance.

In the social sector, quality is a factor in the rent differentiation system. Rent prices per dwelling are calculated using the differentiation system taking into account the required overall rent revenue of the municipality. In this system, elements such as size, standard of equipment, etc., are taken into account.

## III. EASTERN EUROPE

### Bulgaria

The private rental sector uses a maximum rent price per square metre of useful floor space. The amount varies according to the degree of urbanization:

(a) Large cities            2 leva

(b) Medium-sized cities    1.6 leva

(c) Other cities            1.5 leva

(d) Villages               0.8 leva

In addition, the rent price can be corrected according to quality by a factor of minus 50 per cent to plus 20 per cent. Elements accounted for in the quality check include:

(a) Residential location in the municipality;

(b) Type of dwelling;

(c) Floor level within the building;

(d) Useful height of rooms;

(e) (Main) geographic orientation;

(f) Technical equipment (water supply, sewage, central heating, elevator, etc.);

(g) Storage facilities.

The basic rent of State and ministerial dwellings is considerably lower: 0.18 leva per square metre of useful floor space. Corrections are made for quality ranging from minus 50 per cent to plus 32 per cent. The quality check is done in the same way as in the private sector.

## Czechoslovakia

The price is fixed at a firm amount per square metre of living space, depending on the quality class of the dwelling. There are four quality classes. The standard of equipment is taken into account as a criterion.

## German Democratic Republic

A distinction is made between Berlin and other areas. In Berlin, the rent price is 1.0 to 1.25 marks per square metre of living space; in other areas it is 0.8 to 0.9 marks. Rent differentiation takes place on the basis of quality, evaluated in terms of level of equipment, residential surroundings and the presence of central heating. For dwellings built before the Second World War, rent prices are frozen although there is a quality differentiation.

## Hungary

In 1988, the annual rent price for new buildings in the social sector generally did not reach 1 per cent of the construction costs. In the private sector, the rent prices may not exceed twice the amount of those in the social sector. Rent-price regulation for private rental contracts was abolished in 1989; rent levels are therefore freely negotiated. Until 1988, rent differentiation was based on quality aspects in both sectors. The most important quality aspect is the standard of equipment. Five quality classes have been defined for dwellings:

(a) Equipped with all modern comforts (15 forint per square metre);

(b) Partly equipped with modern comforts (with individual heating) (12 forint per square metre);

(c) Without bath facilities or without toilet (7.5 forint per square metre);

(d) Without bath facilities and without toilet (4.5 forint per square metre);

(e) Substandard (one room) (2.4 forint per square metre).

Corrections may be made to the rent prices on the basis of the following factors:

(a) Location in the settlement (from minus 25 per cent to plus 25 per cent) (this option has very rarely been used by municipalities);

(b) Location in the building (up to minus 20 per cent);

(c) Lack of equipment (up to minus 20 per cent);

(d) State of maintenance (up to minus 50 per cent).

Moreover, for large, old apartments, part of the surface area does not figure in the calculation (dwellings larger than 100 square metres or rooms larger than 70 square metres).

## Poland

The rent price is calculated according to a legal standard amount per square metre of living space, regardless of the lessor's category. A correction for quality is applied to this, namely:

(a) No water supply (minus 30 per cent);

(b) Toilet, bath, gas, central heating (plus 30 per cent per element);

(c) Floor higher than fifth without elevator (minus 30 per cent);

(d) Living space larger than 10 square metres per person, per extra room: an additional charge of 100 per cent on the extra space.

## IV. RECAPITULATION

The question raised was: To what extent does rent-price policy in the various ECE countries take account of dwelling quality, and which quality aspects are featured? The scheme below indicates how quality aspects are reflected in rent-price policies in the various countries.

RECAPITULATION TABLE

**Rent-price policy and dwelling quality**

| Country | Rental sector | Quality criteria |
| --- | --- | --- |
| *Western Europe* | | |
| Austria | Private | When setting rent prices and making adjustments; criteria: floor space and equipment level (4 classes). |
| | Social | *Idem* |
| Belgium | All | *Idem* |
| Denmark | All | *Idem* |
| Finland | All | Rent level of comparable dwellings |
| France | All | In case of rent adjustments (national rent-price agreement); criteria: rent level comparable to other dwellings. |

| Country | Rental sector | Quality criteria |
|---|---|---|
| Germany, Federal Republic of ....... | Private | In case of disputes; criteria: rent level comparable to other dwellings; also rent-level survey. |
| Ireland ..................... | Private "Free" | *Idem* |
|  | Controlled | In case of disputes; criteria: nature, character and location. |
|  | Social | *Idem* |
| Netherlands ............. | All | When setting rent prices and making adjustments; criteria: floor space, type of heating, insulation, kitchen equipment, sanitary equipment, age, garden, dwelling type, residential environment and nuisance factors. |
| Norway ................... | 3 large cities | When setting rent prices and making adjustments; criteria: dwelling size and location. |
|  |  | In case of disputes; criteria: value of dwelling or number of rooms. |
|  | Elsewhere | In case of disputes; as above. |
| Portugal ................... | Private "Free" | *Idem* |
|  | Controlled | When setting rent prices and making adjustments; criteria: age and floor space |
|  | Social | For setting rent prices and making adjustments; criterion: floor space. |
| Spain ....................... | All | *Idem* |
| Sweden ................... | All | When setting rent prices and making adjustments; criteria: floor space, specific features, surroundings, location, number of rooms, type, kitchen, equipment, view, bath, balconies, residential quality, etc. ("rent pooling"). |
| Turkey ..................... | All | In case of disputes; criteria: floor space, location, state of maintenance, proximity to centre. |
| United Kingdom ..... | Private | In case of disputes; criteria: floor space, location, state of maintenance. |
|  | Social | When the rent price is set or adjusted; criteria: floor space, equipment, location, etc. ("rent pooling"). |
| *Eastern Europe* | | |
| Bulgaria ................... | All | When rents are set or adjusted, according to such criteria as surface area, degree of urbanization, location, orientation, type of dwelling, floor level, investment level, upkeep. |
| Czechoslovakia ....... | Social sector | When rents are set or adjusted, according to various criteria: surface area, equipment (four levels). |
| German Democratic Republic ............ | All | When rents are set or adjusted, according to various criteria: surface area, equipment, surroundings, central heating. |
| Hungary .................. | All | When rents are set or adjusted, according to various criteria: surface area, equipment (4 categories), location, garden, maintenance, age. |
| Poland ..................... | All | When rents are set or adjusted, according to various criteria: surface area, water supply, sanitary equipment, gas supply, central heating, floor level, density of occupation. |

# Chapter 5

## RENT-PRICE POLICY AND THE HOUSING BURDEN

### I. PRELIMINARY REMARKS

This chapter deals with policies related to rent prices and the housing charges borne by tenants, on a country-by-country basis. Individualized, personalized rent subsidies are discussed along with the overall development of housing ratios and real rent price in the various ECE countries reporting.

### II. WESTERN EUROPE

#### Austria

In the private rental sector, maximum rent prices reflect the level of dwelling equipment. Thus the rent price is not directly related to tenant income. In the social rental sector, the rent price is defined as a cost-price rent. This price reflects the application of interest (object) subsidies to help cover investment costs. In addition to such object subsidies, there are also subject subsidies. These differ according to whether they are applied to the rental or the owner-occupied sector.

In the rental sector, the subject subsidy depends on household income, number of family members and the reasonable use of floor space. In order to qualify, useful floor area must not exceed 50 square metres, rising by 20 square metres for each member of the household up to a maximum of 150 square metres.

#### Belgium

In the private rental sector, the price is set through free negotiation. There is no policy of control over rent prices.

In the social rental sector, subsidies are used. They are based on income. This applies to both the initial rent price and to any subsequent adjustments. Rent prices are adjusted when there are changes in the tenant's income, the standard income, the cost price of housing or in living costs. Tenants are screened for admission according to income criteria established by the Government. Tenants whose incomes have risen beyond the standard may be required to move to a dwelling in the private sector.

#### Denmark

Policy for the entire rental sector is oriented towards cost-price rents. For the uncontrolled private rental housing market, an increase of up to 8 per cent is permitted.

Interest subsidies are applied to keep rents lower in the social housing sector. Subject subsidies are also applied as lower income groups are assisted by individualized rent subsidies. The amount of the subsidy is fixed on the basis, *inter alia*, of rent price, income, number of children and size of dwelling. Only households with an income below a certain threshold are eligible for such assistance. For pensioners, there is a separate system of individualized rent subsidy. The tenant is expected to pay a percentage of the rent price. For pensioners it amounts to 15 per cent of household income; for other subsidy recipients, it is 25 per cent.

#### Finland

Rent prices in the private rental sector are the result of free negotiation between tenant and lessor. The central Government fixes a maximum rent-price adjustment rate each year, which takes into account cost development. The interest subsidy (low-interest loans) granted by the State for the implementation of a rental housing project affects the rent (and the housing allowance) indirectly by reducing the owner's capital costs. The subsidy is consequently not deducted from the rent itself, but from the costs on which the cost-price rent is based.

There are three systems of subject subsidy:

(*a*) Overall rent subsidy for families and individuals;

(*b*) Rent subsidy for pensioners (part of the basic pension);

(*c*) Rent subsidy for students living independently (an extra allowance tied to the student loan).

The subsidy level depends on various criteria: number of household members, household income (both gross and net), personal wealth, dwelling location, year of construction, housing expenses. Only housing expenses that are considered reasonable for a dwelling of a given size are subsidized. Around 30 per cent of all households occupying rental housing receive these subsidies.

#### France

In the private rental sector, the rent price is the result of free negotiations between tenants and lessors. In the social sector (HLM), the Government uses interest subsidies to fix a low rent price. The aim of this policy is to keep rents low in the social sector.

Rent increases for both private and social rental sectors are agreed upon in the national commission of tenants and lessors. If no agreement can be reached through this commission, the Government may set a maximum rate of increase. In principle, adjustments in rent prices are rarely considered a governmental instrument for influencing shifts in the housing burden.

Both rental sectors—private and social—have recourse to a system of personalized subsidies. The amount depends on income, household size and actual rent. Around 45 per cent of tenants in HLM dwellings and 37 per cent of tenants in the private sector benefit from such subsidies.

## Federal Republic of Germany

In the private rental sector, rent prices are arrived at by free negotiation.

Property-related subsidies are paid in the State-assisted housing sector to reduce tenants' burden of housing costs to a tolerable level. Assisted dwellings are only allocated to households whose incomes do not exceed certain limits at the time of approval. The subsidies are reduced over time, or cease to apply when the owners have reimbursed their subsidized loans. This leads to corresponding increases in rent levels.

In addition to the property-related subsidies in the publicly-assisted rental sector, there are household-related subsidies applicable to both the rental and the owner-occupied sectors. The amount of the subsidy is determined according to level of income, size of household, size of dwelling and rent level. Beyond certain rent ceilings, no subsidies are granted. On average, the subsidy covers approximately one third of the rental charges of households; the average rent-to-income ratio, after receipt of the subsidy, is about 20 per cent.

## Ireland

Rent prices in the private sector are set by free negotiation between lessor and tenant. In the social rental sector, price is strongly influenced by the income of the tenant. The rent price is calculated on the basis of the income of the chief wage-earner, according to a scale which runs from one twentieth to one seventh of disposable income. The schedule is adjusted annually, taking into account inflation and the financial position of the municipal lessor.

## Netherlands

Rent prices are set and adjusted freely, but in case of conflict the price may be checked against a point system which indicates a reasonable quality:price ratio. Rents of State-aided dwellings depend initially on construction costs. "Trend" increases guide the rent-price adjustments in line with a maximum percentage increase for a given quality-to-price ratio. The trend takes into account several factors, including effects on the development of purchasing power.

Subject subsidies are also applied. For the entire rental sector, the amount of the subsidy granted depends on household income and the actual rent price.

## Norway

Rent policy for all sectors is similar in that there is no direct relation between rents and changes in the cost of housing. There exists, however, a subject subsidy for inhabitants of owner-occupied and rental dwellings. The extent of the public contribution depends on the characteristics of the household.

## Portugal

In the private rental sector (both free and controlled), there is no fixed link between rent price and housing burden. In the social sector there is a subject subsidy system. The difference between the rent price paid by the tenant and the actual cost rent (determined according to a formula) is paid by the Government. Tenants whose incomes are three times lower than the national minimum income are eligible for subsidies. Income is considered to be the gross salary less a deduction of one twelfth of the minimum income per child. The amount of the rent price paid increases as income thus defined rises.

## Spain

In the private rental sector, a distinction is made between subsidized and non-subsidized dwellings. The rent price of the latter type is, in principle, freely negotiated. For subsidized dwellings, the rent price is fixed at 6 per cent of construction costs. Lessors receive an object subsidy enabling them to set a lower rent.

Rents in the public housing sector amount to 3 per cent of construction costs. This heavily subsidized housing is earmarked for lower income groups. There are, in addition, subject subsidies allocated to tenants with very low incomes.

## Sweden

In both the social and private rental sectors, rent prices are set and adjusted by collective negotiations. Interest subsidies are used to lower the initial rent-price level in both the private and social sectors. These subsidies are gradually reduced over the course of time and rent prices borne by the tenant rise according to a schedule.

In addition to the object subsidy mentioned, there are three forms of subject subsidy. In size, the largest is the municipal housing burden subsidy, allocated as a supplement to the pension for the aged. Over half of all pensioners (800,000 persons) receive this subsidy. Under the two remaining subsidy categories, around 400,000 families receive a subsidy based on income and number of family members; a fixed annual amount per child is granted. Secondly, there is the combined State/municipal subsidy which takes into account income and the housing burden. For the latter, a minimum and maximum rate is established and eligibility depends on household size as one factor. Overall, about 39 per cent of all households in Sweden benefit from individualized rent subsidies.

## Switzerland

Rent prices in the private sector are, in principle, freely set. In the social sector, the rent level is determined by the State (see chapter 3, Switzerland). The initial rent price is fixed at 5.1 per cent of the construction costs. The difference between the initial rent and cost rent is covered by the so-called *Grundverbilligung*. This loan is available to all strata of the population regardless of income and wealth.

For low-income groups, an additional subsidy is granted, the so-called *Zusatzverbilligung*. Households with an annual income of less than SwF 37,000 and a fortune of less than SwF 110,000 are entitled to this aid. This supplementary assistance is provided in two forms: the *Zusatzverbilligung I* amounts to 0.6 per cent of the investment costs and is paid over 10 years; the *Zusatzverbilligung II* is double, i.e. 1.2 per cent of the investment costs, and applies only to elderly, handicapped persons, those in need of nursing and persons on vocational training, provided the income limits are checked.

## Turkey

In the private rental sector, the rent price is established, in principle, by free negotiation between lessor and tenant. In the social housing sector, the rent price fixed depends on the size of the community in which the housing is located. Rents may rise by 15 per cent annually unless otherwise stated.

Admission criteria to qualify for public housing benefits are based on household income for one to two people. This limit may rise depending on household size. Households with low incomes and many children have priority in obtaining dwellings in this sector.

## United Kingdom

Rents in the private sector are set and adjusted regardless of the tenant's income. No object subsidies are granted to lower the general rent level.

In the public housing sector, the municipality collects a rent revenue which varies according to the contribution made by the national Government. In recent years this contribution has diminished. The rent price for a dwelling is determined according to a formula which takes into account the overall revenue necessary for the exploitation.

Tenants may qualify for a "housing benefit" subsidy, depending on their income level. There are two types of subsidy in this category: standard housing benefit and certified benefit. The former consists of a rebate on the rent price for tenants in the social housing sector; the latter consists of individualized subsidies and addresses tenants in the private rental sector. The rebate and subsidy levels are determined on the basis of data concerning the revenue of the lessor, the household composition of the tenant, and the rent-price level.

The certified housing benefit forms part of the public assistance policy and serves as a safety net for those who would otherwise fall below the poverty line despite other subsidy measures.

## III. EASTERN EUROPE

### Bulgaria

For both the private and social rental sectors, rent levels are related to housing quality. Rental policy is aimed at keeping rents low and stable. To this end, substantial object subsidies are provided; in the social housing sector especially, rents have tended to remain very low. Municipal dwellings are allocated by order of priority to those in greatest need. The same criteria apply to dwellings administered by the ministries which are let to public service employees.

### Czechoslovakia

The rent price in both the public and private sectors is fixed at a firm tariff per square metre of floor space, depending on the quality class of the dwelling. Revenues from rents are expected to cover, on average, half of the running costs (excluding capital charges). The remaining costs are borne by the State. The average housing burden ratio is around 4 to 7 per cent of disposable income. The rent share in the total housing burden is less than 50 per cent.

### German Democratic Republic

Rent levels in both the social and private sectors are set so that the ratio of the rent paid by tenants ranges between 3 and 6 per cent. This low level is achieved by the use of State subsidies which cover approximately two thirds of the total costs. Officially set rent prices apply to all rental dwellings irrespective of the tenants' incomes. Large families (three or more children) benefit from a rent subsidy if the cost of housing (including water, heating, and energy) exceeds 3 per cent of household income.

### Hungary

Rents in the social sector are set according to a system of quality classes and cover 1.8 per cent of the construction costs. The quality class depends on dwelling equipment. For each of the classes, there is a basic rent per square metre adjusted according to quality variations. Between 1 July 1983 to 1 July 1988 the rent price doubled and occasionally tripled to a point at which rents now cover running costs (excluding capital charges).

A similar adjustment method is applied to the private sector where the rent price may not exceed twice the amount charged in the social sector. Pensioners and large families with many children may receive subsidies depending on household income, number of occupants and equipment level of the dwelling.

### Poland

Rent price is calculated according to a basic tariff per square metre of floor area with rebates or increases depending on dwelling quality. Rent levels are kept low by means of object subsidies; in 1983 such subsidies covered around 22 per cent of the running costs (excluding capital charges). During the period from 1983 to 1985 inclusive, rent prices were increased to a point at which they would cover 100 per cent of housing costs. Following the 1983 increase, the ratio of rent price to average income was 5 per cent.

Rent price also depends on dwelling occupation density. The basic standard is 10 square metres of floor area per person. For extra space beyond this standard there is a 100 per cent surcharge. Thus, in addition to dwelling size, household size has a decisive bearing on the level of rent charged.

## IV. MACRO-ECONOMIC HOUSING RATIO AND REAL RENT-PRICE CHANGES IN WESTERN ECE COUNTRIES

The macro-economic housing ratio is the quotient of all housing charges and total national consumer spending. This indicator, however rough, shows the development of the housing burden over the years. The macro-economic rent quotient (the ratio of rent to income of occupants of individual dwellings) would certainly yield a more precise picture but such information cannot be extracted from available data.

One constant element stands out in the analysis of overall rental policy: all countries considered in this paper have reported an increase in the share of the housing burden assumed by consumers. The degree of the increase in consumer spending on housing varies widely. For example, Austria, Denmark and the Netherlands show a rapidly rising trend in the macro-economic housing ratio for the period from 1970 to 1984. While the increase has been constant since 1980 in Austria and the Netherlands, in Denmark the ratio has tended to level off somewhat. In Finland, Switzerland and the United Kingdom, there has been a very slight increase in the macro-economic housing ratio. Figures 20, 21 and 22 show the macro-economic housing development ratio, differentiated according to high, medium and low rates of increase in the countries reporting.

In order to show the extent of the impact of rent-price development on the rising macro-economic housing ratio, the real development of rent prices is illustrated in figures 23, 24 and 25. This trend line is obtained by a calculation that comprises the rent index (reference year 1970 = 100) and the consumer price index, both corrected for inflation.

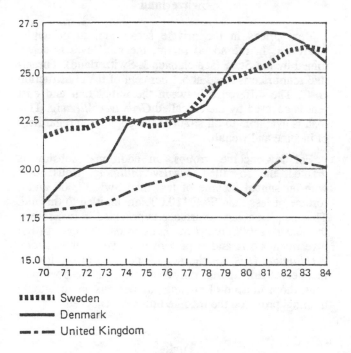

Figure 20

**Macro-economic Housing Ratio
Development 1970-1984
High rate of increase**

ıııııııı Sweden
——— Denmark
— · — United Kingdom

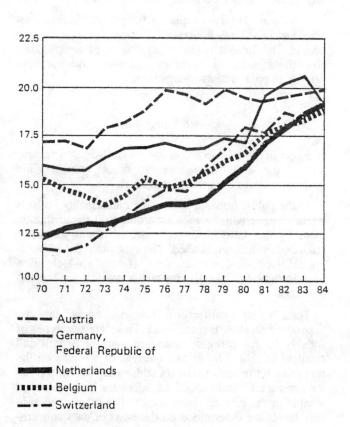

Figure 21

**Macro-economic Housing Ratio
Development 1970-1984
Moderate rate of increase**

— — Austria
——— Germany,
　　　Federal Republic of
████ Netherlands
ıııııı Belgium
— · — Switzerland

Denmark, for instance, has experienced a real decrease in rent prices along with a strongly rising macroeconomic housing ratio. Energy charges are thought to be the decisive factor in this progression. Austria and the Netherlands have undergone a rapid increase (figure 23). In the United Kingdom, a modest change in the macroeconomic housing ratio was coupled with a strong rise in real rents. Owing to a reduction of subsidies in the social rental sector, the housing burden ratio has increased steeply. Meanwhile, the rate of change in the owner-occupied sector has stagnated in relation to the development of housing costs in that sector.

FIGURE 22
Macro-economic Housing Ratio[1]
Development 1970-1984
Low rate of increase

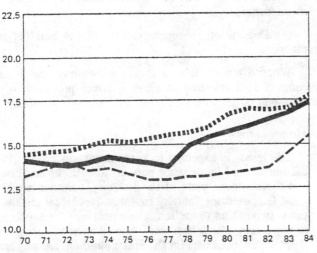

[1] For Finland, the Macro-economic Housing Ratio has been fairly constant over recent decades. It was 17.9 per cent in 1985.

 France
Norway
Italy

FIGURE 23
Real rent prices 1970-1985
High rate of increase

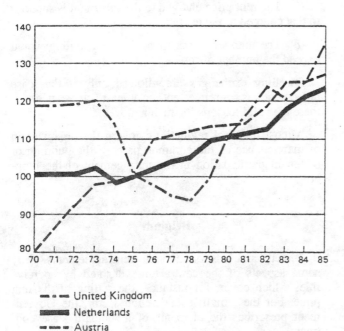

United Kingdom
Netherlands
Austria

FIGURE 24
Real rent prices 1970-1985
Stable

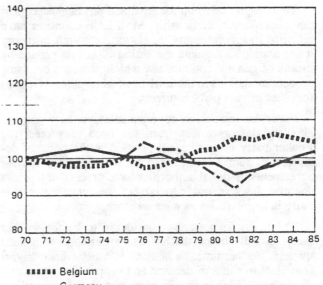

Belgium
Germany,
Federal Republic of
Switzerland

FIGURE 25
Real rent prices 1970-1985
Decreasing

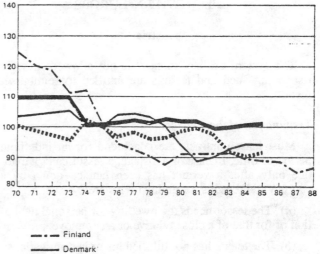

Finland
Denmark
France
Sweden

## Chapter 6

# RENT LEGISLATION

## I. PRELIMINARY REMARKS

This chapter takes up the legal and juridical aspects of the tenant/lessor relationship. Most ECE countries have recourse to special rental legislation, although in theory it is possible to regulate the letting of housing space by means of general contract law which provides the same process modalities in the settlement of disputes as it does for other private party contracts.

Particular legislation covering relations between tenants and lessors arises from the need to protect the weaker party in an unequal position at the point of departure in rent negotiations. As with labour/employer agreements, national authorities have proceeded to enact coercive laws in order to protect the more vulnerable party in negotiations on a lease contract.

The tenant is normally considered to be the weaker party. Usually he or she has less experience with legal matters. Furthermore, as housing is a basic necessity, it is subject to shifts in demand and supply if not to actual shortages. Under such circumstances the likelihood increases of an unequal distribution of powers, with attendant social risks. There is a need to distinguish between supplementary legislation and coercive law in this regard. Supplementary legislation covers points which have not otherwise been stipulated. Coercive law prescribes contract elements which the parties are obliged to honour. Normally, deviations from strict adherence to a contract renders it null and void.

## II. WESTERN EUROPE

### Austria

The system of "key money" is not allowed. Lessors risk being sued and tenants are entitled to reimbursement.

*Termination of the contract*

Most lease contracts are concluded for an indefinite period of time. In case of a dispute, a lessor can give notice only after a verdict has been handed down by a court. Valid reasons for giving notice are:

(*a*) The lessor needs the dwelling for personal habitation or for that of a close relative or an employee;

(*b*) The tenant has not fulfilled his or her obligations;

(*c*) The tenant has died and other members of the tenant's family do not urgently need the dwelling;

(*d*) The rent revenue, inclusive of maintenance charges, does not suffice to cover the cost of decent maintenance;

(*e*) Demolition or reconstruction of the building is planned.

When a tenant dies or leaves a dwelling, the lease contract is transferred to close relatives provided they form part of the tenant's permanent, common household.

*Maintenance*

The lessor is expected to keep maintenance up to local standards. Maintenance pertains to both the dwelling and the common parts of the building, common equipment (e.g. elevator, laundry room) and technical installations. In addition to the rent, the tenant may be expected to pay a levy which becomes a contribution to a share of the maintenance costs for the entire building. Lessors are obliged to carry out maintenance work covered by this levy within five years. Failure to do so entitles the tenant to reclaim with interest any contribution already paid. Lessors must furnish tenants with an annual statement of rent revenue, maintenance expenses and administrative costs.

The tenant may sublet the dwelling unless otherwise stipulated. Revocation of this right is possible only if:

(*a*) The tenant intends to sublet the entire dwelling;

(*b*) The rent price charged to the subtenant is superior to that charged to the tenant;

(*c*) The number of occupants of the dwelling would exceed the number of rooms.

Dwelling exchanges are allowed only if the lease agreement has been in effect for at least five years and if there are valid reasons for such a move.

Almost no legal regulations govern the organization of maintenance of the common parts of the building or of tenant participation in the management of the property.

### Belgium

Tenants and lessors negotiate rent agreements. Only some aspects of the contract are dictated by coercive rules which cover, for instance, the setting of the rent price. For the (small) social rental sector, the Government prescribes the elements of a standard lease contract.

### Termination of the lease agreement

Since December 1983, it has been possible to cancel unilaterally a lease contract which had been contracted for an indefinite period. Grounds for termination of the contract were not specified. A lessor is required to give six months' notice.

The lease contract running for a definite period expires at the end of the contract period. Agreements with a duration of three months to one year are automatically prolonged unless the contract has been rescinded one month prior to the expiry date. In the event of illness, death of a family member, pregnancy or loss of employment, the tenant whose lease was due to be cancelled can appeal to a court for a one-year extension of the lease contract. If the leaseholder dies, the lease is taken over by the heirs, unless the contract otherwise stipulates. Tenants may transfer their rights under the lease contract, partly or wholly, to a third party unless this provision is expressly precluded by the terms of the contract. However, the initial tenant still remains answerable to the lessor for all obligations under the contract.

### Maintenance

The distribution of maintenance tasks is agreed upon by both parties to the contract. Lessors are legally bound to assume responsiblity for major repairs, upkeep of the roof and façades as well as outside painting. The tenant is obliged to take care of the remaining maintenance tasks and make any small repairs. Disputes which the parties themselves cannot solve may be brought before a court. The judge may call experts to hear their opinion before handing down a decision.

### Tenant participation

In the private rental sector, tenant participation in housing management is not specified in law; however, tenants who are jointly responsible for maintaining the shared space in apartment buildings may distribute the tasks among themselves by common consultation. In the Walloon district, in the social housing sector, a decree has provided for the establishment of an advisory committee of tenants and owners. This committee is kept informed of all relevant information by the real estate company managing the building.

## Denmark

The private rental sector and the social rental sector have separate but similar legal systems. In the non-profit, social sector, there are firm prescriptions regarding the rights and duties of lessors with respect to tenants and their participation in the decision-making process. In the private sector, lease contracts must be approved by the responsible ministry, thus the basic rights of tenants are protected. In the absence of a lease contract between the two parties, the stipulations of a model agreement apply.

### Termination of the lease agreement

On the lessor's side, termination of the contract, other than upon its expiry, is possible only on the basis of a limited number of legal provisions, namely:

(a) If the owner needs to occupy the dwelling;

(b) Demolition of the dwelling;

(c) Non-payment of rent;

(d) Misconduct;

(e) Neglect of the dwelling by the tenant.

Family members are entitled to continue the lease contract in the case of divorce or death of the tenant.

Contracts of limited duration become unlimited contracts if the tenant is still occupying the dwelling one month after the expiry of the lease. This is so whether or not the lessor agrees to the continuation.

Subletting of parts of the dwelling is permitted, but the lessor is entitled to 15 per cent of the revenue from the subtenancy. Subletting of the entire dwelling is allowed only in small buildings (blocks of fewer than 13 dwellings) and for a maximum duration of two years.

### Maintenance

The lessor is responsible for most maintenance; equipping the dwelling is the affair of the tenant. However, some other distribution of duties may be agreed upon. If the lessor neglects proper maintenance, the Government may intervene in the management, although this happens only in extreme cases. Disputes between tenant and lessor (e.g. over rent increases or notice to vacate) may be heard by a special legal board.

### Tenant participation

Since 1975, rules have existed governing the participation of tenants on the boards of housing associations. Sometimes such boards consist of tenants only, sometimes of the municipality, trade unions or other groups. In the private sector, in complexes of more than 12 dwellings, tenants are entitled to be represented. The lessor is obliged to consult tenant representatives concerning rent prices, energy savings, maintenance, etc.

## Finland

The Rent Act prescribes the form and content of the lease contract. A lease may be concluded for either a definite or indefinite period. If the duration is less than six months, the agreement may be terminated unilaterally. A contract for a term longer than six months provides the tenant with the same protection as an agreement for an indefinite period. The notice for the termination of a lease contract is six months if the contract has existed more than one year; otherwise it is three months.

### Termination of the lease agreement

The court will agree to a request to terminate the lease if:

(a) The lessor needs the dwelling for personal habitation or for that of a close relative or an employee;

(b) The sale of the dwelling is essential in order to enable the lessor to purchase a dwelling for personal habitation;

(c) There is an equivalent special reason (e.g. modernization);

(d) In the case of student housing, if the academic term has ended;

(e) In the case of employee's housing, if the employment contract has been terminated;

(f) In the case of non-fulfilment of the tenant's obligations (e.g. arrears in rent payment, negligence of maintenance, subtenancy without consent).

If the tenant is unable to find substitute accommodation, the court may grant a stay of eviction for a maximum of one year. Such a delay is not accorded if the tenant has not fulfilled his or her obligations or if the lease contract is tied to an employment contract.

In the case of the sale of a property, the new owner assumes the lessor's rights and obligations under the lease contract.

Subletting requires the consent of the lessor. The original tenant remains entirely responsible *vis-à-vis* the lessor. The end of the lease contract between lessor and tenant automatically terminates any contract between tenant and subtenant.

The lessor is obliged to hand over the dwelling in good condition to the tenant in accordance with local practice. If the dwelling does not meet minimum standards, the tenant can claim a lower rent price or have the deficiencies repaired at the lessor's expense. The tenant is obliged to keep the dwelling in good condition and to take care of maintaining the interior (wall-coverings, painting, etc.). The owner/lessor is not under obligation to indemnify the tenant for any improvements made which have not been previously agreed upon.

### Tenant participation

The participation of tenants in the management of housing has not been codified by any legislation; however, experience in this field has been positive.

## France

The lease agreement must specify the space let, the price, terms of payment, date of rent adjustment and deposit or guarantee sum. The lessor may also be obliged to provide a copy of the house rules. Corporate lessors must offer lease contracts with a periodicity of at least six years. Private individuals may choose between three- or six-year contracts.

### Termination of the lease agreement

In the case of a six-year contract, the lessor may insert a clause laying claim to the dwelling for personal use before expiry of the lease. Upon expiry, the contract is usually renewed for at least another three years. Reasons for refusing to prolong the lease contract are:

(a) The lessor wishes to sell the dwelling (in such a case, the incumbent tenant has the right of pre-emption);

(b) The lessor requires the dwelling for personal use or for that of close relatives;

(c) The tenant has not fulfilled his or her obligations (e.g. arrears in rent payments or neglect of the dwelling).

The renewed lease has the same force as the original one, with two possible exceptions. As already mentioned, a private lessor may insert a clause laying claim to vacant possession of the dwelling for personal occupancy before termination of the lease. The second exception concerns the rent price, which may be altered.

The lease may be terminated by either the tenant or the lessor according to circumstances set out below. Members of the tenant's household are entitled to continue the contract following the death of, divorce from, or sudden departure of the lease-holder, provided they shared the dwelling with the tenant for at least one year prior to the transfer. The tenant may transfer his or her interests under the contract to another tenant only with the express permission of the lessor. Any exchange of dwelling requires the consent of the lessor. Sublets must also be approved by the lessor whether the space concerned amounts to part or all of the dwelling. The rent price calculated per square metre of floor space must not exceed the rent price paid by the original tenant.

### Maintenance

The owner is obliged to hand over the dwelling in good condition to the tenant. The tenant is responsible for daily maintenance and upkeep, and for leaving it in an equivalent state upon vacating it. The tenant's obligations with respect to maintenance are prescribed by law. All other repairs are at the expense of the lessor. When a tenant leaves, an inventory is made to determine the state of the premises.

### Tenant participation

Rules govern consultations between tenant and lessor at residential-complex, county and national levels. Associations of tenants and lessors meet in national commissions dealing with rent agreements as well as disputes. Each region has a similar commission. Consultations at the level of the building complex are defined by law, which sets out the conditions to be met by the tenants' associations for them to be considered as rightful representatives. Lessors hold consultations with tenants' associations on the management of the building complex at least once every three months. The lessor shows them the documentation (bills and contracts) relevant to the running of the building.

Agreements between lessors and tenants may cover:

(a) Control of rent changes;

(b) Improvements and upkeep of common spaces;

(c) Activities promoting social and cultural exchange;

(d) House rules.

## Federal Republic of Germany

Tenancy agreements can, in principle, be concluded in verbal or in written form. However, the latter is the more usual. A verbal tenancy agreement is as binding as a written contract. Verbal agreements are concluded for indefinite periods; they cannot be terminated before the end of the first year. The sum required from the tenant as a guarantee may not exceed three months' rent. The tenant must be given the opportunity to pay the amount in three instalments. Interest accruing on the guarantee is refunded to the tenant upon his departure.

*Termination of the lease agreement*

A lease contract for a fixed term is automatically terminated on the expiry date. Termination before the end is not possible unless proper notice has been given. Most leases run for an indefinite term. Notice must be given in writing to terminate the contract. Both tenants and lessors are required to give notice should they wish to rescind the contract; the length of the notice period depends on the length of the contract. If the latter is less than five years, the notice period is three months. After the tenant has occupied a dwelling for more than five years, the notice period is extended to between six months or one year. The one-year period applies if the lease contract was concluded 10 or more years prior to the period of notice. Although the parties may agree on a shorter period of notice, such stipulation does not apply to the lessor. In the case of a serious breach of contract (misrepresentation of facts, misconduct, arrears in payment of rent) the notice period may be waived.

Cancellation of the lease in order to increase the rent price or sell the dwelling as a vacant unit is not possible. The lessor may terminate the lease contract before the expiry date only if an interest of paramount importance is served. The law provides for three such reasons:

(*a*) Serious breach of contract on the part of the tenant (repeated arrears in rent payments; behaviour not in line with house rules, etc.);

(*b*) Dwelling is required by the lessor for personal habitation or for family members. In the case of a change of ownership, the new owner cannot invoke this claim for three years;

(*c*) Continuation of the lease contract constitutes a heavy financial burden for the lessor.

The court, when considering a request to revoke a contract, may take into account the personal circumstances of the tenant, which would include age, illness, pregnancy, etc. In the case of the death of the tenant, the contract may be continued by members of the tenant's household; otherwise the tenancy is passed on to his or her heirs. In the latter case, either tenant or heirs can terminate the lease contract at short notice. In the case of the sale of the dwelling, the new owner takes over the lease contract made by the previous owner.

*Maintenance and improvement*

The lease contract usually ascribes simple maintenance work to the tenant. This includes painting, papering, etc. Non-fulfilment of obligations on the part of the tenant entitles the lessor to claim indemnification. If the lessor does not carry out the maintenance work which is his or her responsibility, the tenant is entitled to a decrease in rent price.

In general, the tenant is expected to tolerate any inconvenience caused by renovations or improvements. However, the lessor is required to give two months'

warning before work begins and must indicate any effect that improvements will have on the rent price. Annual rent-price adjustments are allowed amounting to 11 per cent of the cost of improvements made (after deduction of any public subsidies and costs of normal maintenance work carried out simultaneously). As an alternative, in accordance with the "comparative rent system" in force, after modernization, rent prices may be raised to the level of similar dwellings in the vicinity.

*Subletting*

Subletting requires the approval of the lessor. However, if the tenant has valid reasons for subletting space in the dwelling (e.g. need of nursing care) the court may authorize subtenancy. The court may overrule the objections of the lessor even if the objections are considered reasonable. However, the lessor is entitled to claim a surplus rent in such cases.

## Ireland

There are very few rules covering lease contracts for furnished dwellings in the private rental sector. It devolves on the parties concerned to agree on the arrangements including rent price, rent increases, termination of the lease and any eventual subtenancy. Contracts are usually for a short term. If a tenant has remained for 20 years without interruption, he or she thereby acquires certain rights. In the event of a dispute, the court may fix a rent price (to apply for five years) and refuse termination of the contract. It is assumed that very few tenants have sought recourse to such a procedure.

Tenants in furnished private rental dwellings (built mainly before 1940) have extensive protection. A special public body may decide a fair rent price. If the family has occupied the dwelling for at least 20 years, the tenant, the tenant's spouse and other members of the family are entitled to protection against eviction. The lessor may only oblige the evacuation of such a dwelling for a limited number of reasons, which include arrears in rent payments. The tenant is not allowed to sublet the dwelling.

In the social housing sector, because of the special subsidy conditions, different rules apply. The municipalities are obliged to fix a certain rent price and dwellings are let according to a standard lease contract whereby the lessor is responsible for maintenance and repairs, with the exception of light repairs and upkeep such as painting and papering. Subletting requires the consent of the lessor.

*Termination of the lease agreement*

In general, the modalities for cancellation of a lease contract are covered in the contract itself.

*Maintenance*

The lessor is responsible for major repair work and for outside maintenance; the tenant is expected to take care of the interior.

*Tenant participation*

There are no express rules governing this, and it may be assumed that tenants seldom take part in decisions concerning the daily running of rental housing.

## Netherlands

Similar rules cover lease contracts in all rental housing sectors. In general, contract conditions in the non-profit sector favour tenants more than those in the private sector. Any system of key money is illegal. By law, the sum held as a guarantee is limited to twice the amount of the monthly rent price. Upon termination of the lease the lessor is obliged to refund the deposit with interest. Subletting of part of the space is permitted unless the parties have otherwise agreed. When the contract between the lessor and tenant expires, any subtenancy contract is likewise rescinded automatically. An exchange of dwellings must be approved by all parties concerned. If the lessor withholds approval, the tenant has the right to seek a court decision. The court may give a negative ruling if it appears that the tenant would not be able to afford the rent price of the dwelling thus acquired.

*Termination of the lease agreement*

Lease contracts for both definite and indefinite periods give almost equal protection to tenants. Contracts are usually concluded for an indefinite period of time. In cases brought before the courts, the possible grounds for terminating a contract are:

(*a*) Failure to fulfil obligations on the part of the tenant, or hindrance to other tenants;

(*b*) The lessor needs the dwelling for personal use (but not just to have vacant possession in order to sell it unoccupied or to let it to relatives). Further conditions are:

(i) The lessor must have owned the dwelling for at least three years;

(ii) The tenant should be enabled to find comparable accommodation elsewhere;

(iii) The lessor should pay an allowance for the tenant's removal costs.

Urgent personal use also includes provision for renovation;

(*c*) The tenant does not agree to a reasonable change in the lease, unrelated to alterations in rent price;

(*d*) Evacuation is required because the land on which the building stands has a new function according to local land-use plans (re-zoning).

A notice period of three months is accorded to the lessor, except in the case of vacation dwellings or official residences (connected with employment). For each year that the lease has run, the notice period is extended by one month, up to a maximum of six months. The tenant is required to notify the lessor one month before terminating the lease. No contract can contradict these terms.

In case of sale of a rental dwelling, the new owner is obliged to continue the lease contract. If a tenant dies, rights of succession to the contract are inherited by the surviving spouse. In the case of divorce, the courts may decide which party shall have the right to remain. Cohabitation implies, by and large, the same rights as marriage with regard to tenancy.

*Maintenance*

The lease contract usually puts responsibility on the tenant to carry out minor repairs and simple maintenance (e.g. painting and papering). The lessor arranges for the remaining maintenance work, although tenants and lessors may agree on some other distribution of tasks. If the tenant is charged with work normally forming part of the lessor's obligations, this should be reflected in the rent price. If the lessor neglects proper maintenance, the courts may authorize the tenant to carry out the work at the lessor's expense. Furthermore, the municipality may oblige the owner to maintain the premises as required.

In the case of serious neglect of maintenance, the rent price may be frozen or even lowered. With regard to home improvements, tenants and owners may agree on a division of responsiblity and cn the impact which this will have on the rent price. The tenant cannot be compelled to accept home improvements unless the lessor's interest in systematic improvements prevails over that of the tenant. If so, the court may call for tolerance on the part of the tenant.

*Tenant participation*

Social lessors are obliged to give tenants the opportunity to become involved in the management of their dwelling although in practice such participation is not very common. Since most social lessors are an association according to the legal definition, members of the management board have a considerable voice in the building's affairs.

## Norway

Tenants may seek a court judgement to obtain more favourable conditions if the rent price appears excessively high.

*Termination of the lease agreement*

Most contracts are concluded for an indefinite period; in 1981, the figure was 90 per cent. If a tenant terminates a contract running for a definite fixed period, the lessor has the right to claim continuation of the rent payments until expiry of the contract. The lessor must give the tenant written notice before terminating a lease. The tenant has 30 days in which to appeal to a court for a judgement on the eviction notice. The court may reinstate the lease if the cancellation is deemed unreasonable.

The lease may be transferred to another tenant without the lessor's permission upon the death of the contracting party. Thus close relatives who formed part of the household of the deceased have the right to assume the benefits and obligations. In the case of divorce, either spouse may continue the contract. Dwelling exchanges require the consent of the lessor.

If housing is leased, the user is entitled to sublet the dwelling for up to two years during the lease period. The lessor is responsible for all maintenance, including painting and papering of the interior although by common agreement the parties may divide their obligations otherwise. In practice, tenants care for the interior and lessors for the exterior. If the lessor neglects to perform maintenance, the tenant may claim compensation.

### Tenant participation

Tenants may take part in the management of the housing estate when the lease contract so provides.

## Portugal

### Termination of the lease agreement

A lease contract is valid for six months unless otherwise specified. Upon expiry, the agreement automatically continues unless notice has been given in writing at least 15 days prior to the expiry date. Thus a lease may be terminated only upon prior written notice. Lessors also may serve notice at the end of the contract period if they wish to terminate the agreement. A tenant over 65 or one who has occupied the dwelling for 20 years or more may not be evicted. If neither party serves notice within the stipulated period, a new six-month contract begins. After one year, the prolongation period is one year.

The tenant only has to inform the lessor before terminating the lease. The lessor may terminate the contract before the normal date of expiry in the case of:

(a) Arrears in rent payments;

(b) Use of the dwelling by the tenant for other than residential purposes;

(c) Alterations by the tenant to the dwelling without the lessor's consent;

(d) Absence by the tenant for over one year.

### Transfer of the lease

In the case of the death of the leaseholder, the contract may be transferred to the spouse or to direct descendants who had constituted part of the common household for at least one year. If there were no cohabitating family members, persons sharing the dwelling for at least five years on an economic basis or subtenants are entitled to a new contract. In the case of divorce or of conflict over continuation of the contract, the court decides.

### Maintenance

The owner is responsible for maintenance arrangements. Failure to carry out essential maintenance allows the municipality to requisition the dwelling, either upon its own initiative or at the request of the tenants. If the municipality does not intervene in such a case within 120 days, tenants themselves may make the necessary repairs. The municipality indicates the amount which may be spent to this end. When the work is complete, the dwelling will be returned to the owner upon payment of the costs incurred.

Home improvements may be done either upon the initiative of a tenant or the lessor. The tenant must bear in mind the obligation to deliver the dwelling to the lessor in its original state, unless the parties concerned have agreed otherwise. Since 1982, through rent-price increases, the lessor is allowed to charge the tenants the costs of improvements allowed for under the lease contract.

### Subletting

The consent of the owner is necessary before a dwelling may be sublet. The tenant may not charge a higher rent for the premises than the rent price prevailing under his or her own lease arrangements. When the lease has expired, the subtenancy also ends. In the case of an entire dwelling being sublet, the lessor may seek a court decision to hold the subtenant responsible in place of the tenant.

## Spain

For the protection of the tenant, public law limits contract freedom. Lease contracts are invariably for an indefinite term.

### Termination of the lease

Tenants may terminate a lease if they observe the prescribed notice period. The lessor may terminate a lease only by a court order in the absence of common consent. Reasons for giving notice to vacate include:

(a) The lessor requires the dwelling for personal use or for that of close relatives;

(b) The dwelling must be demolished to make way for a new building;

(c) The dwelling remains unoccupied for more than half of the year;

(d) The tenant has at his or her disposal, in the same neighbourhood, one or more other dwellings;

(e) The dwelling has become a slum.

Despite the relevance of one or more of the above conditions, the lessor is still under certain obligations with regard to notifying the tenant to leave. The legislation is complicated and the procedure time-consuming, a difficulty compounded by the absence of a tribunal to settle specific rent disputes.

In the case of the death of the leaseholder, the contract may be transferred to close relatives although this may be done only twice. Subletting requires the express written permission of the lessor. Laws stipulate the rent price and protect tenants renting individual rooms.

### Maintenance

The owner is legally bound to carry out all necessary maintenance work. The possibility exists to fix, in exchange for a rent freeze, a charge of 12 per cent to be borne by the tenant and to cover all maintenance costs. Maintenance paid by a tenant may not exceed 50 per cent of the rent price.

In order to make the letting of dwellings more attractive, a bill has been prepared which will allow an increase in rent prices and enable fixed-term lease contracts to be concluded. Participation of tenants in questions of management of buildings is not covered by a public ruling.

## Sweden

For all categories of rental conditions, the same rules apply. Key money is illegal.

### Termination of the lease agreement

Lease contracts normally run for an indefinite period. Contracts of limited duration exist but as soon as a tenant has occupied a dwelling for nine months, the same security of tenure is accorded as to tenants with contracts of indefinite duration. Lessors must give three months' notice. A lessor may force termination of the lease only if a regional rent tribunal considers the reasons valid, that is, for arrears in rent payments or misconduct, etc. If evacuation of the dwelling is required for renovation or because the dwelling is needed for the lessor's personal use, the tenant must be provided with comparable substitute housing. Tenants must observe the terms of the contract when giving notice to vacate their dwelling.

### Subletting

For the subletting of the entire dwelling, the owner's consent is required. The rent tribunal hears the owner's reasons for refusal and pronounces a verdict. In the event of divorce or other changes in the household's situation, the lease may be transferred to other members of the household. Dwelling exchange is possible only on solid grounds and without prejudice to the lessor. As for subtenancy of part of a dwelling, there is no legal obstacle except that it must be without prejudice to the lessor.

### Maintenance

Tenants are not under any obligation with regard to maintenance and must only refrain from causing property damage. The cost of maintenance and equipment of the dwelling (including kitchen equipment) is accounted for in the rent price. If a lessor does not fulfil the obligations assumed under the lease contract, the rent tribunal may call the lessor to account on behalf of the tenant. There were objections to this practice on the grounds that tenants had little influence on their own housing situations. In 1975, therefore, tenants were accorded the right to carry out minor maintenance work without having to seek the lessor's approval. During the period from 1984 to the end of 1986, an experiment was under way to transfer maintenance duties to tenants, simultaneously lowering the rent price.

### Tenant participation

The first step towards greater influence by tenants in the management of the housing operation was taken in 1974 when tenants collectively obtained the right to participate in matters concerning renovation. Since 1978 tenants' organizations have been entitled to demand to be consulted on questions concerning living conditions.

Disputes may be heard by central bodies at which all parties are represented.

In 1979, work started on participation agreements between tenants and lessors; these agreements provided tenants with the right to obtain information on all relevant areas of concern and to influence the decision-making process. Housing associations were organized according to areas comprising 100 to 500 dwellings. Each area had a commission of officers obliged to convoke tenants to meet at least twice a year.

## Switzerland

Regulations related to the rights of the tenant are laid down in two laws:

(a) The general regulations on renting are part of the civil law and are incorporated in the Code of Obligations. These provisions are mostly non-mandatory. The circumstances which are regulated include: change of tenancy, duties of landlords and tenants, subletting, termination of tenure and protection against notice;

(b) The Federal Law on Measures against Abuses in the Rental Sector (Federal Law against Abuses), introduced in 1972, complements the stipulations set down in the Code of Obligations. It mainly contains regulations on notice and on the level of rents.

The principle of freedom of contract underlies the provisions on the rights of tenants and landlords. Since almost all the regulations contained in the Code of Obligations are non-mandatory, changes in and modifications to the standard law are in fact quite frequent in leases. However, in the Federal Law against Abuses a number of regulations have been declared mandatory.

Since written leases play an important role, many attempts have been made to develop a skeleton lease and have it declared universally imperative by the Federal Government, as provided for in the Constitutional Amendment of 1972. At the federal level, these efforts have not been successful so far. But a number of these basic leases have been established at the regional level.

The Federal Law against Abuses is based on the principle that the lease and in particular the rent can be agreed upon freely by the parties. The Federal Government refrains from intervening in the determination of rents. The tenant can, however, challenge the rent and other claims made by the landlord if he believes they are inappropriate. The tenant can take the dispute to an office of arbitration. These institutions are organized to put the tenant and the landlord on an equal footing. They have the legal duty to reach agreement on all problems occurring in connection with leases. If agreement is not reached, the matter can be taken to court. In about 80 per cent of all cases filed so far, the parties have come to terms. Cantonal governments are responsible for the organization of the offices of arbitration and no expenses may be charged for the proceedings.

The key regulations of the Federal Law against Abuses concern the definition of abusive rents. Rents are inappropriate when they yield an exorbitant profit or when they are based on excessive property purchase prices. A rent can also be judged inappropriate when large cost reductions have not been passed on to the tenant. The regulations are designed to ensure the landlord a reasonable return without allowing the tenant to become the object of speculative practices.

To illustrate its meaning, the law enumerates a series of cases in which rents are not considered abusive: as a rule, rents comply with the law in the following cases:

(*a*) When they are comparable to those which prevail for similar dwellings or offices in the same place or district, taking into account location, standard, condition, and age of the building.

(*b*) When rent increases are based on increases in costs or improvements made by the landlord. An increase in mortgage interest is clearly an increase in costs. The regulations cover in detail how an increase in mortgage interest can be passed on to the tenant. Further admissible cost increases are higher taxes, insurance premiums, maintenance expenses and other incidental costs.

(*c*) When rents cover operating costs in the case of new buildings. Excessive land, construction and purchase costs may not enter into account.

(*d*) When rents serve to secure the purchasing power of down payment. As a rule, 40 per cent of the total investment is considered down payment. Thus, rents can be adapted to cover up to 40 per cent of the rise in the consumer price index.

(*e*) When rents correspond to the recommendations of the basic lease agreed upon by the associations of tenants and landlords.

Current regulations differ greatly from earlier solutions, which were based on the principle that rents should not be higher than is necessary to cover operating costs. Taking into account rents prevailing for similar dwellings and offices in the same place or district, present regulations represent a compromise between the principle of free-market rent and that of purely cost-covering rent.

### Termination of the lease agreement

According to the Code of Obligations, courts can defer the notice of a lease-termination in cases of hardship (sickness, old age, a comparable apartment cannot be found, etc.), i.e. when the notice places the tenant in a difficult position which cannot be justified even with due consideration for the interests of the landlord. However, mere reference to a general shortage of inexpensive housing does not provide sufficient grounds for the application of the hardship criterion. No extension at all is granted when the landlord claims the dwelling for his own personal use or that of close relatives, or in the case of the tenant breaking the lease. A first extension must not exceed one year.

In addition, the law contains a number of amendments with regard to the termination of leases:

(*a*) Notice must be given in writing;

(*b*) The landlord may not threaten a tenant with notice in connection with the demand of a higher rent;

(*c*) The landlord may not give notice during arbitration or legal proceedings in court concerning matters of tenancy;

(*d*) The landlord must for two years refrain from giving notice when an agreement has been reached through arbitration, and when he has lost his case in court.

In December 1986, the Swiss people and the cantons approved an amendment to article 34 (protection of tenants) of the Federal Constitution. Accordingly, the Federal Law against Abuses has been in force since 1 October 1987 in the whole country. The entire legislation regarding tenure is at present being revised by Parliament. The purpose of this revision is to make the Federal Law against Abuses an unlimited Federal Law, and to strengthen protection against notice.

### Subletting

Subtenancy is allowed unless the lease agreement contains a stipulation forbidding it.

### Maintenance

The lessor is obliged to deliver the dwelling in the state agreed upon in the lease contract and to keep it in good repair. Failure to do so gives the tenant the right to make small repairs at the expense of the lessor. The lease normally stipulates the elements which are the responsibility of the tenant. The tenant is not allowed to make alterations to the premises without permission from the lessor. By prior agreement, the tenant may be compensated for improvements made.

## Turkey

### Termination of the lease agreement

Contracts are concluded for both fixed terms and for indefinite duration. When subletting a dwelling, the tenant may not charge the subtenant a higher rent price than that paid by the tenant to the lessor. Subtenancy ends at the same time as the expiry of the lease between tenant and lessor. If the entire dwelling has been sublet, the lessor may appeal to a court to have the subtenant take the place of the original tenant.

Lease contracts established for a definite period are normally of one year's duration. If the tenant refuses to leave at the end of the contract period, the lessor may call on a court for an order to vacate the dwelling. The fixed-term contract is converted into one of indefinite duration if the lessor fails to notify the tenant about the termination or expiry of the lease.

In certain areas, in particular in the larger cities, a regulation prevails which offers the tenant greater protection against eviction in the case of temporary lease contracts. Grounds for termination of the lease include:

(*a*) A written engagement by the tenant to vacate the dwelling;

(*b*) The dwelling is needed by the lessor for his or her personal use or for members of the family (applicable after expiry of the lease agreement);

(*c*) The owner wants to renovate the dwelling (upon expiry of the lease);

(*d*) The tenant has twice in a given year ignored exhortations to pay the rent;

(e) The tenant or tenant's spouse possesses a dwelling in the same city.

Upon the sale of a dwelling, the new owner can terminate the lease contract in order to have the dwelling for personal use. The tenant must be informed of such an intention within one month of the date of purchase.

Dwellings in the public housing sector are let for a period of five years, with the exception of official residences. The latter must be evacuated once the employment has been terminated.

### Maintenance

The tenant is required to keep the dwelling in its original state and to do small repairs. The owner is responsible for repairs made necessary by normal aging or caused by catastrophes. The tenant must prove that the damage was not his or her fault. If the lessor neglects proper maintenance of the premises, the tenant has the right to seek a court verdict obliging the lessor to reduce the rent price.

### Transfer of the lease

In the private rental sector, before subletting part of the dwelling, the consent of the lessor must be obtained. In some regions, subletting is allowed if it is without prejudice to the lessor. Upon the death of the leaseholder the lease may be taken over by the remaining relatives who formed part of the household of the dead tenant. In the public rental housing sector, subtenancy is excluded and the contract cannot be transferred following the death of the leaseholder.

## United Kingdom

### Termination of the lease agreement

A municipality or housing association can evict a tenant only if a court order has been obtained. The grounds for this are:

(a) Non-payment of rent or non-fulfilment of the lease;

(b) Nuisance to neighbours or use of the dwelling for illegal purposes;

(c) Damage to the dwelling, its furnishings or to commonly shared parts of the property;

(d) Concluding a lease agreement through fraudulent or false declarations;

(e) Refusal to quit temporary, substitute housing upon completion of work on the original dwelling leased.

If decent substitute housing is available, the court may allow notice to be given if:

(a) The dwelling is overcrowded (1957 Act);

(b) The lessor wishes to demolish the dwelling or to carry out work on adjacent property and must secure vacant possession of the dwelling in question;

(c) The lessor is a registered charitable organization and continuation of the tenant's occupation conflicts with the objectives of that institution;

(d) The tenant occupies a dwelling adapted to handicapped persons and the lessor needs the dwelling for a handicapped person, it being understood that the incumbent tenant is not handicapped;

(e) The lessor is a housing association caring for people with special needs, and requires the dwelling for such a candidate whereas the incumbent tenant does not match this qualification;

(f) The dwelling belongs to a nursing association and is needed for a related purpose whereas the tenant does not need nursing care;

(g) The tenant has inherited the lease through rights of succession and the dwelling is larger than reasonably justified by the size of his or her household.

In the private rental sector, the tenant's protection is less rigidly defined. Lease contracts running for a definite period may be terminated upon expiry of the lease or if the parties wish to terminate the contract sooner. If the contract was for an indefinite duration, there is a notice period of three months for the lessor, and four weeks for the tenant. A tenant may appeal to a court for an extension of the lease.

Further reasons for giving notice to vacate a dwelling include:

(a) The lessor let the dwelling reserving the right to occupy it personally at a later date;

(b) The space had been let for a fixed term of 8 months or less and the dwelling had been let as a holiday residence during the preceding 12 months;

(c) The housing had been let for a fixed term of one year or less and during the preceding 12 months it was let to a student;

(d) The dwelling had been earmarked for habitation by clergy but was let temporarily to another tenant;

(e) The dwelling had been let on the basis of a "shorthold tenancy" and the period agreed has expired.

The contract normally becomes null and void if:

(a) The tenant is in arrears with payment of the rent or has neglected other obligations under the contract;

(b) The tenant causes annoyance to the neighbours or uses the dwelling for illegal or immoral purposes;

(c) The tenant is damaging or allows damage to be done to the dwelling or its equipment or furniture;

(d) The tenant has transferred the dwelling to another party or sublet it wholly to another party without the lessor's consent;

(e) The tenant has ceased to be the lessor's employee and the lessor requires the dwelling for another employee;

(f) The lessor needs the dwelling for personal use or for that of members of the family and the notice given is fair, unless the tenant occupied the dwelling before the lessor purchased it.

For private lessors occupying the same building as the tenant, notice to vacate is less complicated.

*Subletting*

Tenants living in dwellings run by the municipality or housing associations may sublet the dwelling with the approval of the lessor. Such permission cannot be refused unless there are serious grounds for doing so. The tenant may appeal to a court for the decision to be reviewed.

A tenant in the private sector may sublet all or part of a dwelling unless this is expressly excluded in the lease contract. The tenant is obliged, under penalty of a fine, to inform the lessor in writing within 14 days of the start of the subtenancy, stating the rent price charged to the subtenant. Subtenancy of the entire dwelling requires permission from the lessor.

*Transfer of the lease contract*

In the private rental sector, upon the death of the leaseholder the lease contract is automatically transferred to the spouse, or to family members living for at least the last six months with the leaseholder. Upon the death of the successor, the contract is automatically transferred to the second successor under the same terms. When the second successor dies, the lease contract comes to an end.

In the public housing sector, the contract may be transferred to the partner or to family members sharing the same household upon the death of the leaseholder. Cohabitation must have lasted for at least one year. There is no provision for a second successor.

## III. EASTERN EUROPE

### Bulgaria

Since 1969, special legislation has been in force to balance any inequalities between lessors and tenants. Dwellings in the public housing sector are let for an indefinite period even when the lease is connected with a fixed-term employment contract. Private individuals usually engage in fixed-term lease contracts.

*Termination of the lease agreement*

In cases where a court terminates a lease contract, the lessor is obliged to arrange substitute housing for the tenant. Exceptions include:

(*a*) Non-payment of rent;

(*b*) Misconduct;

(*c*) Property damage;

(*d*) Acquisition/ownership of a house.

Termination of a lease in the case of an official residence does not oblige the employer to find substitute housing if both parties have agreed to this action, or if the termination is the result of dismissal for disciplinary reasons.

Contracts between private individuals end upon expiry of the contract. The lessor is not under any obligation to arrange substitute housing. If private individuals let a dwelling for an indefinite period, termination of the rental agreement can only be ordered by a court and eviction is possible only if substitute housing is found. If the owner needs the rented space for personal use, then the rule regarding substitute housing does not apply.

*Maintenance*

The tenant is obliged to look after maintenance and to repair any damage. Upkeep of common, shared parts of the premises also devolves upon the tenant. If the lessor makes improvements to the dwelling (for example, the installation of central heating or an elevator) then the rent may be increased. Municipal authorities are charged with the task of periodically examining the state of maintenance of dwellings in the public sector.

*Subletting*

Subtenancy requires the consent of the owner.

### Czechoslovakia

The law has laid down rules for the content of lease contracts. All lease contracts are valid for an indefinite period. An agreement may be terminated at any time by mutual consent. Tenants may give notice in writing one month before vacating a dwelling.

*Termination of the lease agreement*

In certain situations (e.g. demolition of the building) the court can terminate the lease contract. The tenant is entitled to adequate substitute housing in such a case.

*Subletting*

Subtenancy of part of a dwelling and dwelling exchange are permitted if the authorities so agree. Subletting of an entire dwelling is not allowed.

*Tenant participation*

Participation of tenants in the management of their housing has been provided for by legislation. It is carried out by commissions chosen or elected by the tenants.

### German Democratic Republic

Only dwellings that are in good technical condition and equipped with heating facilities may be let. Equipment must be in good working order. A lease contract may be concluded only if the body in charge of housing distribution so agrees. Failing such consent, the lease is not valid. The rent legislation does not distinguish between public, non-profit or private rental sectors.

Lease agreements must be set down in writing; a standard contract form is usually used. Reference in the contracts to house rules varies from one housing complex to another, but stipulations regarding order, safety and hygienic conditions can only be altered after consultations between the lessor and all the tenants involved.

*Termination of the lease agreement*

Most lease contracts are for an indefinite period. A lessor cannot notify a tenant to leave without a court order. Moreover, the body in charge of housing distribution must also give its consent because substitute housing has to be found.

Reasons for giving a tenant notice include:

(*a*) The dwelling is needed by the lessor for personal use or for that of close relatives (taking someone in for nursing or for being nursed constitutes "own use");

(*b*) Non-fulfilment by the tenant of obligations, arrears in rent payments, neglect of maintenance. If social conditions constitute the reason for non-payment of the rent, arrears are not sufficient grounds for the termination of a lease. However, the tenant may be assigned a cheaper dwelling in such a case.

A tenant wishing to vacate a dwelling should give notice in writing and observe the notice period of two weeks.

Tenants must tolerate dwelling improvement if such work takes place at the initiative of the public authorities. Co-operation on other forms of renovation is not compulsory. The tenant is free to improve the dwelling without the lessor's consent provided there is no question of basic technical alterations. If the lessor refuses to grant the tenant such permission, the tenant may turn to a court for a verdict. Amenity improvements may be transferred by the tenant to subsequent tenants.

*Subletting and exchange*

A tenant may sublet part of a dwelling without permission from the lessor. Sometimes a permit is needed within the framework of housing distribution. The Government encourages dwelling exchange. Such transfers of rights and duties from one tenant to another are expected to be put in writing. Permission must also be granted by the body in charge of housing distribution. Furthermore, this body can compel the lessor to co-operate with the exchange.

*Maintenance*

The lessor is responsible for the technical state of the dwelling and for the proper functioning of equipment. Small everyday repairs and painting are the responsibility of the tenant. Tenants must report any defects immediately to the lessor. Deficiencies which impinge for long periods on the proper functioning of the dwelling lead to a rent rebate.

## Hungary

Lease contracts are generally concluded for an indefinite period. It is of course possible to arrange a fixed-term agreement that expires on a predetermined date. When a fixed-term contract has run more than 30 days beyond the expiry date with the consent of the lessor, the contract becomes a lease of indefinite duration. Fixed-term lease contracts are found mostly in the private sector.

*Termination of the lease agreement*

Lessors may terminate contracts on certain grounds, such as:

(*a*) Non-payment of rent or non-fulfilment of maintenance obligations;

(*b*) Misconduct on the part of the tenant or members of the tenant's household;

(*c*) Damage to rented space;

(*d*) Hindrance to necessary repairs;

(*e*) Dwelling needed by the lessor for personal use or for that of a close relative.

In the latter case, the lessor has to offer the tenant another vacant dwelling in the same municipality. If a tenant does not accept the notice to vacate, the lessor may appeal to a court which may grant an eviction order on the condition that the lessor compensates the tenant for removal costs and also pays—in case of a higher rent price—the difference between the previous and the new rent.

A tenant can terminate a lease by giving the lessor notice in writing and observing the notice period of 15 days.

*Maintenance*

The lessor is responsible for the maintenance of the dwelling, the installations and common amenities. Dwellings owned by public bodies are inspected every three years and any deficiencies noted. In all rental dwellings the same rule applies whereby tenants can appeal to a court if the lessor does not fulfil maintenance obligations. Government policy is aimed at enhancing the role of tenants in the area of maintenance. To this end, tenants are given the opportunity to carry out a considerable part of the maintenance work in exchange for a lower rent price.

*Transfer of lease*

The lease cannot be transferred in the case of official residences or for those connected with employment contracts. Otherwise, the lease may be transferred to close relatives and members of the leaseholder's household. Dwelling exchange requires the consent of the local authorities. No approval is given if the exchange runs counter to the principles of dwelling distribution.

## Poland

The law establishes the relations between tenant and lessor in detail and there is little leeway to conclude any other type of agreement. Only in small municipalities where the owners of one-family houses let part of their buildings does the content of the lease contract (for example, specifying the rent price) play an important role in defining the relations between the parties to the agreement.

*Termination of the lease agreement*

A lease is valid for an indefinite period of time. Lessors must have a court's consent before terminating the lease. Permission is given only under specific conditions, such as serious violation of the house rules. A tenant may serve notice on a lessor provided the dwelling is left in a decent state. In the event of death or divorce, members of the household may remain in the dwelling provided they have resided there for at least two years prior to the change in circumstances.

### Maintenance

The tenant is responsible for the upkeep of the dwelling to the extent that minor repairs and maintenance are his or her duty. The lessor takes care of all maintenance of collective amenities.

### Subletting and exchange

Partial subtenancy is permitted by law if the approval of the owner or manager has been granted. The tenant is then expected to pay a surplus amount beyond the rent price. This provision does not apply if the tenant occupies a dwelling which exceeds the standards and the extra space is let to a student. In particular circumstances, such as a long stay abroad, the tenant may receive permission to sublet the entire dwelling. Dwelling exchanges are also possible and do occur, the only restriction being that the results must be in line with the prevailing policy of housing distribution.

كيفية الحصول على منشورات الامم المتحدة

يمكن الحصول على منشورات الامم المتحدة من المكتبات ودور التوزيع في جميع انحاء العالم · استعلم عنها من المكتبة التي تتعامل معها
أو اكتب الى : الامم المتحدة ،قسم البيع في نيويورك او في جنيف ·

如何购取联合国出版物

联合国出版物在全世界各地的书店和经售处均有发售。请向书店询问或写信到纽约或日内瓦的联合国销售组。

## HOW TO OBTAIN UNITED NATIONS PUBLICATIONS

United Nations publications may be obtained from bookstores and distributors
throughout the world. Consult your bookstore or write to: United Nations, Sales
Section, New York or Geneva.

## COMMENT SE PROCURER LES PUBLICATIONS DES NATIONS UNIES

Les publications des Nations Unies sont en vente dans les librairies et les agences
dépositaires du monde entier. Informez-vous auprès de votre libraire ou adressez-vous
à : Nations Unies, Section des ventes, New York ou Genève.

## КАК ПОЛУЧИТЬ ИЗДАНИЯ ОРГАНИЗАЦИИ ОБЪЕДИНЕННЫХ НАЦИЙ

Издания Организации Объединенных Наций можно купить в книжных мага-
зинах и агентствах во всех районах мира. Наводите справки об изданиях в
вашем книжном магазине или пишите по адресу: Организация Объединенных
Наций, Секция по продаже изданий, Нью-Йорк или Женева.

## COMO CONSEGUIR PUBLICACIONES DE LAS NACIONES UNIDAS

Las publicaciones de las Naciones Unidas están en venta en librerías y casas distri-
buidoras en todas partes del mundo. Consulte a su librero o diríjase a: Naciones
Unidas, Sección de Ventas, Nueva York o Ginebra.

Printed at United Nations, Geneva
GE.90-40607
December 1990–2,595

02300P

United Nations publication
Sales No. E.90.II.E.29

ISBN 92-1-116486-9